Shape-Shifter

BY GAVIN SELERIE AT SHEARSMAN BOOKS

Music's Duel: New and Selected Poems
Collected Sonnets

Shape-Shifter
—a tribute to Gavin Selerie—

curated by
David Annwn

Shearsman Books

First published in the United Kingdom in 2022 by
Shearsman Books
PO Box 4239
Swindon   SN3 9FN

Shearsman Books Ltd Registered Office
30–31 St. James Place, Mangotsfield, Bristol BS16 9JB
(this address not for correspondence)

www.shearsman.com

ISBN 978-1-84861-873-2

ACKNOWLEDGEMENTS

The publisher is grateful to the following: Gavin Selerie for permission to
reprint 'Backstory' which originally circulated privately in an edition of 25
copies; Gavin Selerie and Binnacle Press for permission to reproduce 'That
Dada Strain' from *The Riverside Interviews: Jerome Rothenberg* (Binnacle Press,
1984); Linda Black and Claire Crowther of *Long Poem Magazine*, who first
published Gavin Selerie's 'Long Haul Voices'; Jeffrey Side of *The Argotist*
(online), who first published the full version of Andrew Duncan's interview
with Gavin Selerie as *Into the Labyrinth*, a free PDF eBook; Ian Seed of
Shadowtrain who first printed Ian McMillan's review of *Music's Duel*; David
Caddy of *Tears in the Fence*, who first printed Anthony Mellors' review of
Hariot Double; and Geraldine Monk, for The Estate of Alan Halsey, who
authorised the reproduction of 'A Maze for Grammatologists', first printed
on the cover of *Shearsman* magazine, 1st series, nº 7, in 1982.

Contents

Gavin Selerie

Pictorial treatment of Jerome Rothenberg's 'That Dada Strain'
(text from the New Directions book of the same title).
from Jerome Rothenberg, The Riverside Interviews.

David Annwn

Preface

Due to Gavin Selerie's urgent health issues, it was decided to invite his friends and readers to contribute writings and images to an anthology of responses to his work.

Gavin is perhaps the most celebrated and well-known of English writers creating long Modernist and Late Modernist poems (the latter his own term) post-1970. As he himself writes:

> I seem naturally drawn to structures which involve cumulative and twisting elements. The modernist long poem offers an escape from closure while still allowing progression. There is often a displacement of temporality.
>
> ('Long Haul Voices: the Book Length Poem')

Book-length sequences such as *Azimuth* (1984), *Le Fanu's Ghost* (2006) and *Roxy* (1996) are landmarks in contemporary literature and this poet can just as readily explore smaller, shorter forms in collections like *Tilting Square* (1992) and *Southam Street* (1991), as well as the individual poems of his *Collected Sonnets* (2019) which stand out lividly like spars, strongly individual and yet also inter-related, by pattern and rhythmical structures, to other works.

In terms of context, the poet identifies with the third wave of Modernist and late Modernist writers post the British Poetry Revival, finding himself influenced by structuralism in the 1980s. His work reveals a shape-shifting faculty seen in his doubling and mirroring as in *Hariot Double* (2016) or sudden transformations into new graphic structures as in 'Screen Seen: Reduction' from *Le Fanu*.

Gavin's poetry is often one of sudden displacement, transition, gear-changes and other shifts. Ian MacFadyen kicks off his contribution here with morphing visions of womanhood: 'She shapeshifts from shopgirl to showgirl, from street to stage, catwalk to screen.' Gavin quotes Thomas Sheridan's *Art of Punning* with obvious fascination: 'Rule 14. *The Rule of Transition*: Which will serve to introduce any thing that has the most remote relation to the subject you are upon.' 'Briny Shifts' from *Hariot Double* rearranges passages in Chapman's *Odyssey*. In 'Fire', Ian Brinton evokes bizarre and surreal changes: 'fire shifts like an amoeba as well as like a giraffe'. These transitions are also realised in the paratextual materiality of Gavin's books, as in his carefully-configured and gold-leaf burnished cover for *Tilting Square*, R.B. Kitaj's pastel and charcoal drawing on the cover of *Roxy*, Alan Halsey's cover and lettering for *Azimuth*, the Brinsley Le Fanu picture on the cover of *Le Fanu's Ghost* and also in its deep green endpapers and holographic images, the whole volume masterfully designed by Glenn Storhaug.

Gavin's activities in fostering poetry have never been limited to his mainstream literary output; his series of *Riverside Interviews* published by Binnacle, such as the volume on Jerome Rothenberg (1984) and his occasional festschrifts for his friends such as his *Epithalamion on the marriage of Geraldine Monk & Alan Halsey* (1998) reveal an interest in nurturing international ties and friendships in the arts.

Words from Peter Middleton's essay included here recounting his first meetings with Gavin are indicative:

> He was generous, Elizabethan, Olsonian, enthusiastically immersed in writing and reading poetry, interviewing poets and producing lengthy Binnacle Press booklets, collecting bootleg tapes, and recommending the best of the song lyricists. He introduced me to the 10,000 Maniacs.

That generosity and conviviality are familiar to so many writers gathered here. In his sartorial jackets, sometimes bright shirts and trademark hats, with raffish moustache (sometimes askew with amusement), smile and piercing eyes, Gavin has brought colour to a myriad of literary scenes: a poet on the hoof, liaising, introducing, supporting so many among the different reading venues, pubs, universities, theatres, concert halls and streets, particularly in London but elsewhere too.

There is of course, another side to Gavin: the poet as secret observer and private eye taking it all in, a fan of British Noir films' mystery and enigma. Accompany him in person or follow his writing down any city street and he will open out its secrets and hidden histories: for example the London pubs and hideaways of Dylan Thomas, Julian Maclaren-Ross and Humphrey Jennings.

As many writers comment here, Gavin is also an unashamedly serious and learned author and avid bibliophile with his personal library of perhaps 45,000 books. He has a huge collection of Golden Age detective fiction and the pride and joy of his library is *Camden's Britannia* (first edition in English, 1610). It is worth pausing to compare this in terms of scale with Umberto Eco's collection of 30,000-plus books acquired recently by the Italian Culture Ministry.

In this volume, you will find recollections and poems, visual homages, photographs and essays, interviews and precious hard-to-find items like Ian McMillan's *Shadowtrain* review of *Music's Duel*. Andrew Duncan, David Hackbridge Johnson and Lyndon Davies discuss the poet's love of music. There is discussion of his explorations of Surrealist paintings. Robert Hampson brings in Gavin's affinity with cinema, theatre, architecture and fashion. Mandie Wright writes of their shared interest in folk song. Yet this is no place to pre-empt the pleasure of discovering this book for yourselves. Our thanks to all the contributors for giving so generously of their time, to journal editors for permitting the reprinting of rare articles and to Gavin himself for his invaluable help in compiling this volume.

Laurie Duggan

Paul Nash #2

wind has bevelled these trees
– a beech copse on either hill –

they straddle bounds of a shire
dark masses in low sunlight

against colours of a landscape
where a sunflower turns

for the last light, rolls
as a ball of fire down the slope

Gavin Selerie at a reading (above),
and reading with Frances Presley (below).
Photographs by Laurie Duggan.

Robert Hampson

Gavin Selerie: cutting a track

I have known Gavin as a poet, critic and friend for some 50 years. In the essay he wrote for *Clasp*, Gavin dates the beginning of his 'full engagement' with the London poetry scene to 1978 and his attendance at Eric Mottram's poetry reading series, King's Readings.[1] I might have met him there – or perhaps later at the Subvoicive readings at the White Swan (which ran there between 1983 and 1988). I probably attended the launch of *Azimuth* at the White Swan in June 1984; and I almost certainly heard him read the first draft of *Roxy* there in November 1985. We definitely spoke and drank together in the bar there on many occasions after various other readings.

The earliest of his publications that I came across was probably *To Let Words Swim Into the Soul* (1980), a fine extended essay on Charles Olson, published as an anniversary tribute ten years after Olson's death.[2] In its retracing of Olson's diverse researches, the essay is also a tribute to Gavin's own seriousness as a literary researcher. Gavin returned to that essay's implicit presentation of poetry as a research project in a later essay on Olson in which he cites Olson's 'layered sense of history' and the 'marshalling and deployment of information' as part of Olson's legacy.[3] Together with the creative and expressive use of the page space, these were part of Gavin's own inheritance from Olson.

In that same year, Gavin also published his *Riverside Interviews* beginning with Allen Ginsberg and ending with Tom McGrath.[4] Through such projects (and his research on Renaissance literature), Gavin was carefully laying the foundations for his own career as a poet. His early engagement with sonnets – in *Azimuth* and *Elizabethan Overhang* – did not chime with my interests at that time. I was more interested in his

---

[1] Gavin Selerie, 'Kaleidoscope of Spirits', in Robert Hampson and Ken Edwards (eds), *Clasp: Late modernist poetry in London in the 1970s* (Bristol: Shearsman Books, 2016), 119-30.

[2] Gavin Selerie, *To Let Words Swim Into The Soul: an anniversary tribute to the art of Charles Olson* (London: Binnacle Press, 1980).

[3] Gavin Selerie, 'From Weymouth back: Olson's British contacts, travel, and legacy' in David Herd (ed.), *Contemporary Olson* (Manchester: Manchester University Press, 2015), 113-26, 119.

[4] Gavin Selerie (ed.) *The Riverside Interviews* (London: Binnacle Press, 1980);

use of longer forms. My own early engagement with Gavin's work was through *Roxy* (1996), a ten-year research project that took off from the name 'Roxy' to offer a multi-layered engagement with popular music, cinema, theatre, visual art, architecture and fashion.[5] I was particularly taken with *Days of '49*, his collaboration with Alan Halsey, which was written to celebrate the two poets' fiftieth birthdays.[6] As the title already suggests, this engagement with the year of their birth is not an attempt to recover originary memories, but rather a foregrounding of the layering of memory: this historical layering is signalled in the title, which references the poets' memories of Dylan's 1970 version of a Goldrush song from 1849. The subsequent poems construct a version of 1949 from newspaper reports and through attention to cultural events of that year, but they are consciously seen through the optimism of the late 1960s and the dumping of the post-war socialist dream in the 1980s.

For me, Gavin's major works are *Le Fanu's Ghost* (2006) and *Hariot Double* (2016). *Le Fanu's Ghost* developed out of the 'marginalia procedures' and 'raised documents' of *Days of '49*.[7] It has its basis in Gavin's extensive scholarly and critical work on the extended Le Fanu and Sheridan families and their various writings, supplemented by Gavin's documentation of his on-foot investigations of relevant sites. Gavin layers different historical contexts throughout the sequence, interlinks separate parts through repeated motifs, and engages in constant formal inventiveness. The poem becomes a house haunted by ghosts, but it is also pervaded by Gavin's writerly playfulness. *Hariot Double* was another extended research project.[8] This time Gavin juxtaposes the very different lives of the Renaissance scholar Thomas Hariot and the jazz saxophonist Joe Harriot. There is an element of chiasmus underlying the project: Hariot travelled from London to the New World to explore the colonies in Virginia; Harriot travelled from Jamaica to London to become part of the London jazz scene of the 1950s and 1960s. The volume draws on Gavin's research interest in the Renaissance, his love of jazz and memories of an older London. The project also provided the opportunity for a research trip to Virginia. Again, the volume is marked by Gavin's serious playfulness in its exuberant use of the page space and fertile creation of poetic forms.

[5] Gavin Selerie, *Roxy* (Hay-on-Wye: West House Books, 1996).

[6] Alan Halsey & Gavin Selerie, *Days of '49* (Sheffield: West House Books, 1999).

[7] Gavin Selerie, *Le Fanu's Ghost* (Hereford: Five Seasons Press, 2006).

[8] Gavin Selerie, *Hariot Double* (Hereford: Five Seasons Press, 2016).

In 2001 Gavin wrote the Preface to my *Assembled Fugitives: Selected Poems 1973–1998*.[9] It was as careful and precise and scholarly as one would expect. Gavin concludes by recalling Subvoicive and the London poetry milieu which from which the collection had arisen – and in which we had first met. Gavin himself has been a prominent figure in that world since 1978 – an attentive figure at readings, seminars and conferences, and, indeed, a striking figure with his neat moustache, his penetrating gaze, and something of the dandy in his various hats.

---

[9] Gavin Selerie, 'Preface' to Robert Hampson, *Assembled Fugitives: Selected Poems 1973–1998* (Exeter: Stride: 2001), 9-12.

Harry Gilonis

Horace, *Odes* I.xx
— an Imitation, of sorts, for Mr. Selerie

It's vile to glug small glasses, 'responsibly'
– sooner a twi-handled jug, I'll testify:
fingering the pull on a renegade can
        garners no plaudits.

Gavin, you're a clearly distinguished poet,
sporting, jocose, by fleet banks and, west, bourne's groves
to hear eccho toss'd of Vniuersal shout
        from your Concaue hills.

No *ordinaire* best laid down and avoided
would be fit Poet's Beverage, augment fame;
neither would temperant vices – *such* bad form –
        best honour your name.

*(with grateful nods to John Dunstall [1671], Christopher Smart [1767],
Philip Francis [1853], Edward Dunsany [1947], and the tribune
Gaius Epidius Marullus, fl. 44 BC)*

Frances Presley

Hod Hill

for Gavin

1

startled yellowhammer
through barbed wire

thin nourishment for the ground
fallen branches
fragments of ash
yellow lichen
cow dung
snail shell

crow row day
memory of green
my life just broke again

the bare earth
a slice of skull exposed

these are the healthy parts
the woods

this is the tumour
mown to a blank
harrowed

2

white bark   chalk land
white crusts of dung

puzzled bullock above me
bellowing
an expectation

miniature bulrush
taken back

we bared the earth
and now the earth bares us

only the tall yellow grass
a thin covering of hair

harvested fields
undulating stripes of grey and yellow
I can't wear this
I can't sell this for the walls of a hospital

3

purple scabious
small blue
marbled white on bramble

all these
with the broken chalk
falling hillside

they have chopped trees and bushes here
thorns rising again

stop this conservation landslide
conservative landslide

purple thistle
we can't grow back
but you can

drops of rain already

4

top rampart / hill fort / hod hill / home

rain winding in from the west
winding sheet
don't wait for the rainbow

flicked by swifts
waterfall

5

base rampart

retreat from the grazed heights
poor ash shelter

I cannot unsee the blank space
the chalk
when I wanted to take you to sandstone

written in rain
this cross section of your brain

swifts like armies slice
across the gashed ramparts

chalk and flint
are not grey matter
this is a false analogy, Hazel

kites whistle through hazel
kites cry

September 5 '22

Hod Hill is an Iron Age earthwork in Dorset, inhabited into the Roman and mediaeval periods. The Old English 'hod' could mean shelter or 'hood' – the shape of the hill. It is close to where the annual *Tears in the Fence* poetry festival is held and David Caddy takes visiting poets on a walk around its ramparts. Gavin and I walked it with David in 2020, when it was only the three of us, because the festival had to be held online. Gavin was supposed to be with me this year, but fell ill and a few days earlier we had seen the scan of his brain, a slice of his skull, and the aggressive tumour.

Gavin and I first met on the London poetry scene in the 1980s, sometimes at the experimental and performance series Sub-Voicive. I also saw him perform the wonderful *Strip Signals* at the Musicians' Collective. We fell in love in the 1990s. I was trying to remember happier times and chose a poem from February when we stayed in Ely and walked the surrounding fens. Gavin took delight in the Gothic architecture, while I explored the landscape. It's part of my *Black Fens Viral* sequence, which concerns the ecological disaster of fens drainage, viral assaults and the Markov Chain algorithm. I was also thinking of Geraldine Monk and her Sheela Na Gigs. She was in my thoughts constantly this year, as her husband, Alan Halsey, Gavin's close friend and collaborator, was seriously ill. She too was trying to remember their life together before the illness struck. The walk was a punishing experience and it was an immense relief to find an open church. We hugged the wall for shelter and sat in the sun to eat our sandwiches, feeling like a pagan carving and admiring the rewilded graveyard.

February 22

Cawdle Fen cold spring to spew on us skeletal umbels excitable crows teasel whiskers and hogweed flatten against thorn broken old willow hanging on past all tillage lip fallen rut past all triage insect flattens against the page – hello perfect camouflage flatten against the bank wind whips up glad for a church read open at Little Thetford where gargoyles spew on us skeletal umbels glad for a pew fast against thorn and the gapemouthed graveyard soaking up the unnatural heat flatten against the church feeling the gargoyles tongue to disorder in a common space o a skylark hangs out its tongue fast feeling like a space to be teazelled for they are rewilding the church and feeling like Sheela Na Gig on a low stone teasel and heat with my legs spread open na gigla to disorder

Giles Goodland

The Lamp

for Gavin

Let the hurricane-
lamp in the forest
to which these moths are
drawn to illuminate
and foreshadow the cloth
with the other forked creatures,
winged feelered
pincered and variously
veined, be
the poem. But
the larger beings who
flee from the light:
those with mass, who
mass, jointed
and friendly, lunged,
those with whom we sat
and laughed, those
present to us, most
like us,
how to catch those?

Ian McMillan

Review, *Music's Duel: New and Selected*, from *Shadowtrain*, 2009.

Shearsman is one of my favourite presses because not only do they seek out new and exciting work from all over the world but, like Salt and Carcanet, (and many others) they present us with reconsiderations of older writers, poets who've been publishing for many years but whose work has often slipped under the radar of that odd and unclassifiable beast, the general poetry reader. Gavin Selerie is one such writer: he's been active since the 1970s, mainly in the London poetry scene, and his work reflects influences from the metaphysical poets via Black Mountain and popular culture and found language.

In an essay in *Jacket Magazine* about two of Selerie's collect-ions, *Roxy* and *LeFanu's Ghost*, Robert Hampson describes him as 'probably one of the most obviously scholarly of contemporary British poets' and it's true that collections like *Roxy* are the result of years of research and rewriting, in *Roxy's* case ten years from start to finish, and the collection takes in the history of cinema, Selerie's own life in London, and historical and political events that occurred during the book's gestation; what I like best about Selerie, though (and I hope I'm not being heretical when I say this. Actually, I don't mind being heretical, so ya boo sucks.) is the immediacy of his language, the way he speak directly to me, the way he can illuminate a day with an idea or a line. Take these satisfying stanzas, set in Rosedale in North Yorkshire, an area ringing with layers of history: 'Glass Holes/a little way south/in shale and sandstone//dug for rabbits/yield something else//vessels/from a winged surface/under bracken//pale green beaker pieces,/neck of a wrythen Kuttrolf bottle,/pincered handle from a bleeding bowl, girth of a globular jug/linen-smoothers or slick stones...' Beautiful!

Music's Duel contains extracts from books like *LeFanu's Ghost* alongside uncollected poems from the same decades as the more substantial works, and in the book we see Selerie's development from the earlier pieces quoted above via the longer works to recent uncollected poems, like the moving and ostensibly simple 'Deep Clearance', about the clearing out of (I'm guessing) Selerie's parents' bookshelves, heartbreaking in the apparently workaday language: 'His copy of *The White Company*/with detached boards, signature and address,/ 184 Wardour Street, my own name/appended above.//*Stories from English History,*/my mother's prize, September 1927,/Lady Margaret's School, Willesden Lane./ 'No more wars', says the parson in hope/(last page)'. The poem ends 'all margin/ each book a case of unwritten thoughts', a troubling idea that sends us back into the poem, back into the idea of what reading and writing can be, and how memory can function within that.

And maybe that, in the end, is why I love Gavin Selerie's work so much: he always sends me back into the poem, always makes me work hard even with the apparently simple lyrics. He won't let it lie, he won't let me lie. 'Tomogram', for example, is 'an enquiry into the origins and meanings of 'ghost', including its use in a printing context': 'Your text is the ghost of a call/(I did not ring) but since after all the message yields up//Caxton's H/a panel of ink starvation/as seen in Gothic – 'ghastly for to see'//the word is as much as breath/at three removes//beyond the jurisdiction of veracity/paling in a spectral line...' and so on, each stanza stopping you in your tracks, each packet of information and art forcing you to take your time.

So you can read Selerie on many levels: he's a poet of place, describing urban and rural settings with an accuracy and craft that always illuminates the human engine that drives the visual delights; he's a love poet or a poet of relationships, creating tender lyrics on the longevity of desire, and he's above all a restlessly experimental writer, always wanting to expand the idea of what a Gavin Selerie poem can do, and by extension what all poems can do.

Read this book: you won't be disappointed. If you are, blame me, not him.

Peter Middleton

from A Yearlong Poem Diary

October 10

For Gavin Selerie

I need to say that this is one of many entries from an emerging poem diary. During the course of a month I revisit the same poem on different occasions, and each time record how the light strikes it that day. Parts of it edge into shadow, stubbornly resistant to memory, while previously disregarded lines start insistently calling attention to themselves. Late August and September were spent with Wallace Stevens' 'An Ordinary Evening in New Haven,' and now in October it is the turn of a poem by Douglas Oliver.

Today I am thinking of David Annwn's urgent invitation to write something now, *right now* for Gavin, and how I don't have anything new for him, want to offer some fragment of creative work while all I have is this amorphous journal, and I am conscious that for October I am about to start writing about Oliver's poem, 'The Oracle of the Drowned.' I shall treat Gavin as a welcome guest appearing in this entry, the first on Oliver's poem. Will it be appropriate to do so, I don't know. When I was writing about Stevens, again and again I returned to a self-styled *clou* (it's a poem with several disruptively arcane words), the phrase 'the less legible meanings of sounds,' a line that may be a bridge to Oliver's poem, a line that goes straight to my cochlea. Life-long deaf I have always been conscious that sounds may (or may not) have legible meanings just out of reach. Here in the word *legible* are the inner letters of *elegy*, split into different phonemes, that will be my guide today as I introduce Gavin's poems to Oliver's.

Elegy, eulogy. Leg, legend, legible. Log, logey, éloge, blog.

Oliver *by* the sea. 'The Oracle of the Drowned' presents Oliver's childhood memory of the first time he saw a dead person, a drowned man carried dripping up the beach as he and other children watched, a man whose inchoate ghost then haunted his dreams. A strong childtime experience of the edge of life influences the adults we become, 'as you, a baby, will have a man and call him 'Father' / and as the drowned will have the drowned.'

In Elizabeth Strout's most recent novel, *Lucy by the Sea* (one of those punning titles that children often find funny) the protagonist Lucy Barton mentions that newly dead friends and family always visit her in dreams a few weeks afterwards. Once assured she is alright they don't linger, they're 'in a hurry to get back to dead-land.' I've found this to be true of my own dead. One friend appeared at an airport where he was changing planes, pushing a symbolic shopping trolley with his otherworldly goods in it, hurriedly said a warm hello, then pressed on into the crowds after promising to come back once he'd located his gate. He never reappeared. Another who I thought was still alive was helped out of a low mound-like tent by an inner circle of friends, while I and other more distant friends stood back. Later that week I heard she was in a final coma. My father sometimes appears, never says anything or shows any awareness that he's deceased, just reminds me that he is there with the drowned.

'The Oracle of the Drowned' nearly disappeared into the sea of out-of-print books. It appeared in *Three Variations on the Theme of Harm*, that had the misfortune to be a Paladin paperback whose publishers turned against the series and pulped the books, one of too many instances where radical poetry has been suppressed. Fortunately Ian Brinton recently chose this poem for the new Shearsman *Selected Poems* and it is back in circulation again.

Oliver distinguishes between the imaginary drowning man, and the dead body brought out of the sea. While drowning, the man has the warped articulacy of an ancient oracle, speaking incomprehensible syllables that may be closer to the truth than we can bear. Oliver treats this ghost from his young dreams as a figure representing anyone struggling to hang on to their sanity or soul, while also reminding us that the process of dying can confer a special wisdom on those who move closer to the heart of things.

We ask the dying, 'How do you go about drowning?'
and the answer comes first 'I cannot –'
then swims in ambivalent vowels
and voiceless consonants in the washing tide
voiced consonants in the last buzz of the eardrum:
'Aah, I am funtoosh, zooid, walway,
wallowing, rows and rows of waves,
a goooood one, my soooul a sea-mew' –
and we learn nothing but the knowledge of pain,
and the hope of a future from it.

The first words of the drowning man are unusual, some distorted, some not: funtoosh from fantoosh (extravagantly dressed), zooid (an organism that buds off another), walway (perhaps from while away). Then the *oh* vowel extends its weird aria. To learn wisdom from the dying, says the poem, is like learning to make sense of prophecy. When in 2008 I was high on morphine and dying of a severe spinal infection I felt as if my soul was similar drawn away from the daily world, out on a long thread of life, and only the love of family and friends kept the line from stretching to breaking point. Glimpses of incommunicable wisdom trembled in this distance from the living world. Afterwards for several months I had difficulty connecting visual images on television, and words in oral lectures, as if the communicative world no longer made full sense, its verbal and visual grammars had been severed.

Oliver's oracular distortions of language are similar to what I hear in my damaged ears and in the mouths of those with aphasia. When I speak to Gavin on the telephone after his seizure at first I don't recognise his voice, its instrument has a darker, more burnished wood, and only when he has uttered several sentences do I recognise the personality, the familiar intellectual rushes and darts, the wide modulations are still there. After smaller talk we move on to the grey mass that threatens his mind, and he tells the story of the night when it happened, the crash of change. As Gavin talks his speech begins to burble, disjuncted words and sounds float apart like the elements of a paragram. He calls a halt, we reluctantly say goodbye.

Gavin has created a major body of work. He has been a pioneer of the contemporary history poem, he's written narratives in a dazzling variety of lyric forms that line up into biopics of Lefanu and Sheridan, Hariot and Harriot, and others. Oliver's poem explains that the 'gone-dead' are far more intelligible than the drowning, the already dead make legible sounds, they are 'beamish and talk to us / from out of memory's hollows and gulphs.' Gavin has recognised this illuminating beamishness and asked what it takes to enable those dead creators of our literary history to speak out of the gulphs. His later books, *Hariot Double* and *Lefanu's Ghost*, have the intricate ecology of a tangled bank of literary history.

Both Doug and Gavin were mentors. Doug I saw only rarely, sometimes in Southampton, mostly in Paris. Gavin was a constant guide to scenes of life at the capital and its poetry from soon after I moved to London in 1979. He was generous, Elizabethan, Olsonian, enthusiastically immersed in writing and reading poetry, interviewing poets and producing lengthy

Binnacle Press booklets, collecting bootleg tapes, and recommending the best of the song lyricists. He introduced me to the 10,000 Maniacs, and I listened to *The Wishing Chair* endlessly, fascinated by the way Natalie Merchant articulates the words like Oliver's drowning lyricist in a series of slides and mid-word pauses that stretch and compress the phrases, notably in 'Tension Makes a Tangle': 'But who grants absolution for sins that never were committed … Tension makes a tangle of each thought / becomes an inconvenience / sound as it never penetrates.'

As I think about Oliver's poem, I notice how much Gavin's poems differ in their verbal intensity. His lines are granite in which crystals of meaning have been compressed by immense tectonic forces. Characteristic poems frequently change planes in mid line, just when we think we know where things are heading, a break in the fugue takes us off somewhere else, tugged by an allusion or startled by a dark image. 'Privily,' which concludes *Tilting Square*, warns the reader that the appearance of bared soul in this sequence is sometimes just appearance, that 'behind the wordface is another / made up … subjecting flesh by a sleight / which hides how one leads back to many.'

Sleights of mind? The sonnet 'Waste Zone' pullulates with what Gavin calls in his notes on the *Sonnets* a 'searing irony' directed at the transformation of east London waste land, from a 'weed web' where 'A fruiting body rises purple / from scum or shattered brickwork' out of a dirty ecology adjacent to 'the valley where thrushes, herons, bees / make life,' transformed into the Queen Elizabeth Olympic Park, one of those absurdly over-abundant reminders that we are not citizens, we are supposedly subjects of a democratically unaccountable monarchy. Gavin starts with a comparative view of the Greek originals of the Olympic games: 'It's not a marble thing in wooded hills / to find who'll go to the last ounce of blood / for an olive wreath.' No, though it's a thing alright, its thinginess is made of 'steel tubes / over a concrete bowl' and built on polluted ground. Gavin frequently teases the reader, as he does here, with hints of riddles, less legible allusions, in this case microshock images of bloodshed, hydrochloric acid dumps, and scum. The final couplet of the poem is a rhetorical question: 'Can a smooth track, a push and a scream / fit us right on screen as a legacy bite.' This meniscus of polemical clarity – is the celebration of human athleticism sufficient compensation for what this legacy park has buried? – is gradually poisoned by the harsh nouns, *scream* and *bite*, and a hint of criminal violence ('a push and a scream'), and the sinister idea that all this might 'fit us right on screen.' Gavin may expect us to think of Thomas Kyd's shocking line from *The Spanish Tragedy*, 'Why then Ile fit you,' quoted in *The Waste Land*.

There is rarely an *I* in sight in this layering of image and allegory. Gavin's poetry often starts with a propositionally forceful, surface statement beneath which emotionally laden allusions, sometimes to specific biographical or historical facts, sometimes to metaphorical conceits, reach down into the depths. Statement in his hands has a cutting edge, can be both judgement and flourish. In *Roxy*, in a series of emphatic clauses, Gavin tests out his beliefs about prosody: 'A new metre is a new attitude… An angel rests in a crevice, / runs on the old iambic stroke / or joins the dots that no one sees.' As we are no angels, we may miss the angles, fail to join the dots between the events to which he alludes. His poems measure us. 'All grammars leak,' he tells us, and I nod furiously. Then to demonstrate what he means, adds an enigmatic illustration: 'the end of the silk road / is an animal print shirt / reassuringly dear.'

Reading 'The Oracle of the Drowned' alongside my guest poet Gavin, I see how Oliver likes to be explicit, to keep the drowned and the dead distinct. Gavin lets the drowned and the dead embrace in his poems, speaking with ictus stones and fruiting vowels roiling in the voice, listening to the historical dead who appear to have settled into narratives illuminated by beams of understanding, embracing in the intertidal zone of 'uncertainties, mysteries, doubts.' Neither Oliver nor Gavin are willing to go all the way with Keats, though, and both do reach tentatively and without irritability, for 'fact and reason.'

Leaking, dripping, oceanic grammars.
Legible, elegy, eulogy. Legible, legend, leg, end. Blog, logey, éloge.

Quotations from:
Gavin Selerie, *Collected Sonnets* (Bristol: Shearsman Books, 2019).
———— *Roxy* (West House Books, 1996) sections 35 and 36.
Douglas Oliver, *Three Variations on the Theme of Harm* (Grafton/Collins, 1990).
———— *Islands of Voices: Selected Poems* (Bristol: Shearsman Books, 2020).

Andrew Duncan and Gavin Selerie

From *Into the Labyrinth*: an interview conducted by Andrew Duncan in 2011

AD: I wanted to ask about azimuth and binnacle and whether the navigation theme had to do with Olson.

GS: I've always been a great reader of voyage literature, Hakluyt for example, and always loved going by sea. I went to North America at the beginning of 1968 by a cargo ship from Liverpool to Boston, and as a boy I used to go mackerel fishing in Cornwall. I've been on all kinds of water expeditions and am, incidentally, a water sign. I got quite fascinated with aspects of navigation. So it's the history of moving around from place to place by water and the ways in which people navigate it. Like Olson I suppose I took that as an emblem. Making 'azimuth' the book title is more emphatic. I'm sure I did know about the word from physics or astronomy, but I may have first come across it in an in-depth way with the Pink Floyd. When I went to a concert of theirs on the South Bank in the late 1960s, they used something called an 'azimuth projector', as a way of distributing sound around the hall.

AD: So it wasn't realistic stereo, it was deliberately altered and directed?

GS: I was never a lover of quadraphonic systems, but I think in a hall there are strong arguments for doing something like that. I must have read in *NME*, or maybe *IT* or *Frendz*, about the Azimuth Co-ordinator. Probably Roger Waters would have been holding forth about it. I think they were still using it when I went to see them perform *Dark Side of the Moon* at the Rainbow at the beginning of 1972. Nowadays people regard things like *Tommy* and *Dark Side of the Moon* as clichéd and programmatic in a dull predictable way, but at the time those pieces came out they were tremendously exciting. That *Dark* concert took place six months before the album came out. I suppose I'm mainly interested in earlier Floyd stuff, but the timbre of sound at the Rainbow show, in that setting, was extraordinary, and similarly the light show etcetera. So perhaps I absorbed something of a contemporary sound context for *Azimuth* from the Floyd's Azimuth Co-ordinator. But I didn't decide on the title for that book – although by 1978 it had already become a long poem project – until I went to visit John Robinson, of *Joe DiMaggio*, in Bounds Green, and he played me this LP....

AD: …an exhibit here [LP called *Azimuth* by Azimuth with a photo of the ocean on its cover].

GS: …which had just come out. Which initially I thought was just called *Azimuth*, but it's truer to say this is a group called Azimuth. It's chamber jazz music. It's just a trio: John Taylor on piano and synthesizer, Norma Winstone, voice, and Kenny Wheeler the great Canadian trumpeter on trumpet and flugelhorn. It says released in March 1977 but I know I couldn't have heard this until 1978. There's a lighthouse on the cover, and a lot of these pieces seemed to have the sea or a direction connotation. 'Siren's Song' opens it and then 'O' [or nought] leads into the title track. On side B you have 'The Tunnel', 'Greek Triangle' and 'Naked'. When John played this I was mesmerised to find a song called Azimuth, and I already knew two of the musicians, that is, on record, particularly Norma Winstone. Her first album *Edge of Time* influenced my sense of possible structure a lot because it proceeds from chaos to a sort of lullaby at the end and it showed how *furor* [frenzy, wild excitement] could be joined with a more settled melodic quietness. *Edge of Time* I would think was about 1972. The thing about Norma Winstone, and this happens on the Joe Harriott album *Hum Dono*, which would be something like 1969, is: she sings as an instrument – as the equivalent of a saxophone or whatever. Norma Winstone is one of my heroines and I've stayed with her over the years. She's also on *Labyrinth*, the Nucleus album, which I still find inventive. I heard Ian Carr's group in various incarnations, in Oxford among other places. Winstone sings the part of Ariadne in this suite which is based on the Theseus and the Minotaur story. With this striking cover.

AD: Not really in keeping. Were they on Vertigo? They were trying to sell that kind of thing to a pop audience. Interjecting for the new reader, Norma Winstone was I believe a free jazz vocalist, so completely different from vocalists like Billie Holiday. I guess part of this was to do with producing an English jazz style, it had to purge an awful lot to cease being American at one remove. So improvisation was a big part of it. Most modern poetry comes out of music and this is most obvious with rather banal poetry, it's oriented towards pop song lyrics, people are so used to that. The banality of the lyrics becomes the banality of the poetry. But modern style poetry hasn't really escaped from music, as a welcoming warm and liberated environment. But modern-style poetry has a home in very modern-style music, of which English free jazz and chamber jazz are examples.

GS: There is a poem towards the end called 'Azimuth' which is dedicated to Norma Winstone, whom I finally met after a concert at the Drill Hall in the early 80s. I didn't reprint this in my *Selected* because it doesn't seem to work fully now, but I think I still stand by it. It's about four, five poems from the end:

> This I know to be my way
> plotted first by the wind-rose and the stars
> then by arcs of declination intersected

AD: Could I interject there, this is a guess, that the interest of navigational terms for free jazz was not to do with getting from a known place to a known place. It was actually about being in the middle of the ocean, and you invent your own geography, and your own course, and the point is not losing confidence in what you're doing. Could I suggest that in *Azimuth* the relation with the Pink Floyd sound projection thing is to get away from point and towards an area. *Azimuth* is a very complicated poem and you could say it has a centre in a dozen different places.

GS: I'm glad you brought things back to the aleatory and the non-predictable, because that is my orientation. I got distracted by the concept and the programmatic. I think dislocation – not knowing where you are and having to find your way by whatever means are available, or plotting a course that goes in a circuitous way, a way that includes mishaps and mistakes – is what I was interested in. Although such openness is particularly pronounced in Olson, the long poem traditionally includes digression. Homer, for instance. The long poem, not just the modernist long poem, usually has this twisting vitality. Narrative tends to encourage these fluid, chance or stray elements. But Olson was an inspiration for me in showing how you could utilise diverse materials within a longer text. If you think of the variousness of *The Maximus Poems*, the use of Algonquin mythology, Jung, along with actual voyage journals and narratives. That combination of historical texts with oral legends, their exact status open. Of course it's also the combination of text and observations – walking the streets of Gloucester and nearby territory: Dogtown, Gravelly Hill, Stage Fort *et cetera*. This creates a kind of sliding reality. I think indeterminacy is vital. I mentioned in my email to you that remark of Keats to Reynolds: 'We hate poetry that has a palpable design upon us – and if we do not agree, seems to put its hand in its breeches pocket. Poetry should be great & unobtrusive, a thing which enters into one's soul, and does not startle or amaze it with itself but with its subject.' And then a little bit later on he says 'I don't mean to deny Wordsworth's grandeur, [...] but I mean to say we need not be teazed with grandeur & merit when we can have them uncontaminated and unobtrusive.' Keats is rather out of fashion these days. But that opposition to palpable design is a crucial stance. I suppose it's a truism of Romanticism really, that you don't trust what has come down as a blueprint, you forge your own path, your own meaning. That said, obviously all poets do use design, however free they are. You can't get completely away from design.

AD: So improvisation has its intent. But its outcome may be something that has genuinely shed all genre rules, and a whole tier of consciously known rules, perhaps not all rules of language ever memorised or internalised but a significant part of them. The converse of this is the claim often made that the audience can't understand modern poetry, which in a sneaky way does prove that poetry has gone beyond. Got away from itself.

GS: This may not be directly responding to what you just said, but I think you raised something that preoccupies me: a procedure that moves beyond semantics or which contains a pure sound dimension. I'm interested in this because I'm on the one hand fascinated by commentary and critical interpretations of texts and on the other hand always wanting to return to the text in a purer way. I remember Peter Riley, in his essay in *Poets on Writing*, saying something to the effect that the poem says what it means starkly and the reader is left with that. Poetry says what it says in stark isolation leaving you to make sense of it. This would involve getting away from any appendages, so that the reader finds their way through the text without a crutch, without interpretative props. I think that's a well made point even though I'm fascinated by commentaries such as you get in Sandys' 17th century translation of Ovid where you get marginal glosses and annotation at the end of each book. Even though I'm fascinated by that and always have been, I love footnotes. Ultimately you get back to the fabric of the text and it goes beyond meaning in any detachable sense. The content is in the form as Olson said, quoting Creeley. Actually, the statement in *Projective Verse* is 'Form is never more than an extension of content.' But Creeley develops this in *A Quick Graph*: 'The poem is not a signboard, pointing to a content ultimately to be regarded... It is the way a poem speaks, not the matter, that proves its effect'. The elements are not really separable. We have to negotiate the fabric of the language – ah we're back to 'Azimuth' bearings – in grappling with a poem and coming to a sense of what it means. There is an interesting passage in Puttenham's *The Art of English Poesie* in which he contrasts the art of prose and poetry [pulls book off shelf]: 'The utterance in prose is not of so great efficacy, because not only [is it] daily used, and by that occasion the ear is over-glutted with it, but is also not so voluble and slipper upon the tongue, being wide and loose and nothing numerous, nor contrived into measures and sounded with so gallant and harmonical accents, nor in fine, allowed that figurative conveyance nor so great licence in choice of words and phrases as metre is.' Metre there suggests a very arranged or stress-based form of poetry but I think he is suggesting that poetry has the capacity at least to move onto a purer level of language because it's not so worn. Would you say, Andrew, this is opposite to Wordsworth's emphasis on…

AD: It's not quite symmetrical. He is talking about freedom, and I have to say that modern prose doesn't have quite the qualities he attributes to it, as 16th century prose did, also not all poetry fits into that scheme although it's a very beautiful idea. I think the Objectivists were pretty much marching in the opposite direction.

GS: It's important to bear in mind the historical development of these genres, and Melville's prose for instance is poetry at some level, isn't it. Maybe I've reverted to talking about arrangement as opposed to spontaneity and irregularity. But I think there is a level at which poetry transcends meaning – certainly in the detachable sense – and I don't think you get that so much in prose, although you could argue that any passage of Joyce and Beckett, or goodness even Iain Sinclair now, moves beyond. All poetry is sound poetry at some level, even though the term tends to be used to apply to an extreme of that.

AD: We seem to have defined freedom there, which is very satisfying. I'd like to say that it's not just the poet who enjoys the feeling of freedom and lack of constraint, but the reader as well. The reader is either adrift in this sea of language or swimming, buoyed up by it like a fish in water. I think that's what the Azimuth idea is all about. I suppose it's not the rules of prose which are restrictive, it's the attitude of some readers.

GS: Things go back to how, as a reader, you approach the text, and this is subject to all the variables of experience. You might read something differently on a train from how you would in the privacy of your living room, and you might read something differently performing it, compared to silent reading. I sent you my statement on poetry which was part of my entry on the British Electronic Poetry Site until this got deleted by mistake. [It's now on the Archive of the Now site.] In that I argue for a reclaiming of rhetoric, on the assumption that rhetoric in the true sense is not deceptive or artificial but is literally the best words in the best order. OK, Cicero and so on may have been thinking mainly of argument but rhetoric also involves description and patterns of, the shaping of phrases within a sentence or beyond a sentence. My defence of rhetoric is I think relevant to my procedures in *Roxy*, where I've got a kind of dialectic going on between the regular, the formulaic and the dispersal of intention. In that statement I was saying that sometimes nowadays the experimental becomes a kind of mantra, an obsessive mantra whereby the poet is supposed to shed traditional forms and planned arrangements, and I think rhetoric in the sense of recourse to tried and tested patterns, or useful patterns, is still fundamental to poetry, and people don't want to admit that... .

In your essay on *Azimuth* you expressed considerable reservations if not hostility to *Tilting Square*, my second book of sonnets, and I think this could be germane to the area we were just talking about. In that book I am very sensitive to pattern, and I combine fixity with fluid elements. I'm on the one hand trying to construct a series of interlinked units, and on the other hand moving literally in reaction to what is happening around me and not being predetermined. Those two books came out of my life at the time. *Elizabethan Overhang* comes mainly out of a love affair although I am not just dealing with the subjective. There are more general poems here that intersect with the directly personal. The opening poem ['Make-Up'] is much to do with language as well as the expression of feeling within a relationship. 'First Born' is to do with being first born, the first in a family. 'Tundale' is about the danger of AIDS at one level, and from a heterosexual position. Certainly when I went out to America in 1988 it was a threat to heterosexuals as well. 'Delayed Release' concerns what's happened to the ideals of the 1960s. 'Less and More' engages with the issue of 'the new man', pretty topical in the 1980s. I was just making a qualification there, to the point that both books come out of the personal. Let me grab *Tilting Square*. This juxtaposes an affair I was having with someone who at the time was still married but who subsequently left her husband, with the death of my father which happened during that period. See section 4 which also contains poems about the rest of my family, including my mother. The structure of the book is based literally on the *Tilting Square* images I drew at the time.

Or those visual designs suggest what was also emerging in language. The cover has the design for section 1, with the tip of a pyramid picked out in gold. Actually gold leaf, hugely expensive. This begins a sequence of straight-line shapes within a turning circle. The initial square within a circle is an envelope but also, because of that tip, an incipient pyramid, realized fully in the design for section 5. The intermediate designs feature different configurations, including zigzag or 'vanishing' parts. I suppose the point of that was different configurations within a relationship, or a family, and in society. To some degree this is highly organised and thought out. I think the envelope suggests poems sent by letter, which many of them were, secretly. And the circle, which may also be a ball, could imply energy flow. The images are playful and a serious plotting of life-patterns.

In a general way they were inspired by Paul Klee's notes on related shapes and colours in *The Thinking Eye*. I think he's particularly concerned with figuration in movement, the dynamics of the line. I must get back to the point at issue.

Didn't you react adversely to what you saw as a stiffness of language? Obviously I'm using the sonnet here. I think I could stick my neck out and say that in the *Reality Street Book of Sonnets* mine are among the few which are genuine sonnets. I'm not in any way objecting to the material in that anthology. I think it's a wonderful anthology. What I was trying to do in both these books was to stay close to the Elizabethan and Jacobean, and extend it through to the 17th century and even to the Caroline. That phase of very intense sonnet-writing, although most of the sequences come from the Elizabethan and Jacobean period. I was trying to find an equivalent to that. The fourteen-line form in a sequence whereby motifs are picked up, recapitulated and you get that whole interpenetration between different texts. I was trying to retain that but to find a way of doing it afresh. After Barthes, Derrida and feminist theory – I mean with an awareness of such thinking, not imitation. And, poetically, with a sense of what had been done later, from Barrett

Browning and Meredith through to Cummings, Empson and Berryman. I can now be detached about it and see that I am simply putting too many words into a given text of fourteen lines or into the line. I think Andrew Crozier told me off for doing that, or implied that the lines were too stuffed.

AD: I found it very hard to understand but perhaps a re-reading would have taken care of that. All three of the ones you mentioned seem a lot clearer now. Sorry, who is Tundale?

GS: It's a medieval text.

AD: *The Vision of Tundale*? *Visio Tnugdali* in medieval Latin?

GS: Yes, this includes a vision of the damned, which may have influenced Bosch's *Garden of Earthly Delights*, the triptych in the Prado.

AD: It's related to *The Voyage of Saint Brendan the Abbot* but with a different hero. It is the same voyage. AIDS has to do with paradise lost?

GS: I think perhaps a nightmare journey which confronts you with difficulties. But yes, that would link with other poems, particularly the one in *Elizabethan Overhang* about the 1960s and the effects of that, 'Delayed Release'.

AD: It's on the facing page.

GS: There's obviously a degree of intentionality there. These poems, as well as negotiating that fourteen-line thing, and occasionally using rhyme, are an attempt to grapple with and resolve paradoxes. It's the configuration thing again. The poem 'Numbers', in *Tilting Square*, concerns the relative advantages and disadvantages of being in a couple and being single, and just deals with the look of numbers, which are I think very suggestive. One being a straight form rising upwards, and two being a curved form which may go down and end flatly, or rise up into a curve. If you look at the first stanza.

AD: 'One stands up and two leans back…'

GS: I think I'm wrestling with ethical problems, with physiological problems. These poems were driven by a need to make sense of what was happening at a philosophical level. Maybe the piled-up language comes partly from the fact that I was pressurised but also from this need to think things out in that pressurised situation. The philosophical implications of emotional business. Poems that concern the act of writing ['Make-Up', 'Business and Origin'] juxtapose two levels of effort or involvement, and those that deal with the position of the poet ['Parnassus' and 'Utility'] contrast or draw parallels between the professional and domestic. Longing, attainment, dislodgement.

AD: I think what caused me problems was wondering whether it was a sonnet sequence about one situation with the same two people in so that there is a carry-over of meaning between the different poems. Or whether they were really separate. I think they are quite separate from each other so the problem was perhaps imaginary.

GS: But they are cumulative in terms of theme and effect. As with my long poems the sequences here involve many connections. Some of them would be chance connections obviously. I went through a long period of listening intensively to Renaissance airs, particularly, madrigals too, and using Renaissance song-books, anthologies of sonnets, as back-up.

AD: So we're back with music again!

GS: These come out of the experience of listening to composers like Michael East and John Wilbye. For instance, 'You meaner beauties of the night' and 'Draw on, sweet night'. I was particularly fond of Emma Kirkby's record *Time Stands Still* and Camerata of London's *English Ayres and Duets*. Also the tenor John Elwes. I taped a mass of material from Radio 3 in the 70s and 80s, and my then-colleague Roderick Swanston copied performances of all of Dowland's airs for me. There are poems on Gibbons and Byrd in *Music's Duel*. My take on the sonnet is different from, say, Creeley's reworking of the Campion mode, in that I strive for something more metaphysical. Unlike most songs the language is almost clotted, it's very dense. Whereas with true songs you're getting more of a lyric simplicity.

AD: I think all modern poets were going through something like this in the 1980s. There seemed to be this fetish of titling something 'song', Denise does that, when you couldn't possibly sing it. If it were going to be in a song it would already be there in a song by Campion or Lawes or whoever. The whole point of being a modern poet is that you have been locked out of that paradise and you succeed if you accept that state. So we've got that very exciting new music of the 1960s which has ebbed rather decisively. We've got free jazz, which is almost not there, it's the taste of freedom, out in the ocean. And we've got the Renaissance. None of those actually gives you a way of writing poetry. You have to write it as poetry.

GS: I've got two reactions to what you've just said. But winding back to what we were saying a little earlier, taking forms beyond what they were in their literal context. You mentioned Denise Riley. Coleridge would be an earlier example here with his adaptation of the ballad form for 'The Rime of the Ancient Mariner'.

AD: You couldn't possibly sing that. There is that spooky quality with Coleridge. Then there's 'Christabel' which you could sing. As pastiche it's impossibly good. Incredible. But he couldn't do it consistently, we're talking about two poems in the whole of his lifetime.

GS: [In 'The Ancient Mariner'] he is faithful to the line and stanza pattern of the ballad and to its usual subject context, but does a vast expansion. In the second edition with the marginal gloss as well. So that's one example I wanted to flag up, suggesting the successful expansion of an old form. When I look at *Tilting Square* now and this piled-up, concentrated language, it seems to me that people like Tony Lopez were doing similar things then in terms of density. It must have been something to do with the British cultural climate, but maybe also the influence of LANGUAGE poetry. Getting away from the oral in a strict sense, that 'speech act' which Robert Grenier and others found so suspect. I suppose Prynne's redefinition of the lyric mode was particularly crucial for British poets at this time.

AD: What was the other point you said you wanted to make?

GS: Well, you said 'You have to write it as poetry'. I agree, but isn't it still a negotiation with aspects of music, even if it's dissonant and fragmented? I've referred to a complexity of interlocking ideas and images that take these sonnets away from what is typical in song. But I'm aware that I was still influenced by, say, John Renbourn's setting of the Donne song 'Go and catch a falling star', which I heard him perform with Doris Henderson in the 1960s. I set another Donne poem to music, 'Sweetest love, I do not go', around 1970. Neither of these is a sonnet, I'm thinking of lyric patterns. The melodic line offers fluency with a degree of breakage. This stuff is in my bloodstream and, while I don't wish to repeat what's been practised to death, I like using a model to bounce off. You can set up contrary impulses and conflicting rhythms within a tightly knit or restricted form. It creates tension between the predictable and the uncertain. Going back to the LANGUAGE poetry quarrel with directly oral discourse, this seems to have been part of a reaction against the assumed subject position – the beak of the ego which Olson tried to get away from, with middle voice and so on. I'm slightly eliding the dogmatic with the subjective here. Anyway, Perelman and Bernstein found many of the Olson generation or tradition still culpable in this respect. So you get a shift away from what is, in some ways, still a lyric voice. There is more emphasis on the construction of personality.

AD: Am I not right in thinking that the essential feature of the sonnet sequence was that it was amazingly egocentric and that was part of a Renaissance revolution which was, I suppose, minimising the power of religion. There was no earlier equivalent for extensive poetic works with that degree of egocentricity.

GS: It was highly subjective in terms of romantic experience but that is distanced somewhat by convention, isn't it, as the tropes of Petrarch are recycled endlessly. In England Wyatt did something very individual with the sonnet. However dependent he is on Italian and, in some cases, French sources, there's an absolutely unique forging of language and a refusal to be limited by convention.

AD: You could say that being revolutionary was linked to being individualist... .

Note: the full text of *Into the Labyrinth* is available as a free download from argotist books: http://www.argotistonline.co.uk/INTO%20THE%2LABYRINTH.pdf

This in-depth interview covers Selerie's work up to Music's Duel *and, significantly, includes a full account of the London poetry scene from the late 1970s to the 1990s.*

Allen Fisher

Lugg Mill study
oil pastel on ink wash on paper, 51 x 39 cm (20 x 15 ins)

Gavin Selerie

From *Backstory, the making of* Roxy (1998)

Roxy Section 43

This was inspired by Angela Carter's reminiscence that, as a girl in the Granada, Tooting, she tapped the green marble to see whether it was hard or hollow. I heard her talk about this on a BBC *Omnibus* programme in 1992; the text, dated January 1992, has now been published in *Shaking a Leg: Journalism & Writings* ed. Jenny Uglow, 400. At one level section 43 is an exuberant memorial to Carter, who died in February of that year.

There was a particular vogue for exotic monumental details in cinema architecture in the 1920s and 1930s. The Astoria, Streatham, for instance, had an Egyptian style bas-relief around the circle and curtains which resembled an Egyptian tapestry. The exterior of the Luxor, Twickenham had bell-shaped lotus-leaf capitals and stylized winged heads, while the interior had 'a great bird with outstretched wings flying above the stage' (Richard Gray, *Cinemas in Britain*, 70). The front of the Carlton, Islington had 'bulbous columns, stylised papyrus leaves and pyramidal forms' (David Atwell, *Cathedrals of the Movies: A History of British Cinemas and their Audiences*, 97). The dream palace here is loosely modelled on the Pyramid (Odeon), Sale, as described by Dennis Sharp:

> Here the exterior was fashioned into the form of a pylon – with windows added – and above the entrance doors four columns with hybrid Bell-type capitals carried the neon lettering and the central clock. Inside, the hypostyle auditorium was decorated in Egyptian style in fibrous plaster. Even the [organ] did not escape the desire for stylistic unity and this was decorated with images of Pharaoh's slaves. The consistency of the detailing was remarkable: papyrus and lotus flower forms ran up the side of the proscenium arch, while above the centre of the stage area a winged solar disc spread out its arms as a symbol of protection... (*The Picture Palace and Other Buildings for the Movies*, (123-4)

Sharp provides photographs of the exterior and the interior of the Pyramid, including a picture of the assembly of the organ console, which has Egyptian heads, columns and stepped terraces (ibid., 123-25). Other

Egyptian features are incorporated, leading on to sections 44 and 48. My travels in Egypt are obviously an influence on such description. The joining star-points in a huge grid are a particularly strong memory (see 'Aspic' in *Tilting Square*). There is a family association: my great uncle Bob, who worked for Shell, lived in Luxor.

David Atwell's book contains a wealth of visual material which relates to this section and to section 1, written before I read his study. 'Cathedral of Motion Pictures' was Samuel Rothafel's epithet for the Roxy, New York City. There are photographs of the Astoria, Finsbury Park (67, 82), the Astoria, Brixton (80), the Carlton, Islington (97), the Granada, Tooting (118, 124-5,130-32), and the Granada, Woolwich (140). Dennis Sharp's book is also well illustrated.

Much of the detail in these cinemas has been lost due to reconstruction – particularly at the Astoria, Streatham, which I knew briefly in the late 1970s when I was living in the area. The Luxor has been demolished. My Egyptian cinema is now a cinema of the mind, in some ways appropriately, although the Carlton is relatively well preserved. The Astoria, Finsbury Park, with its Moorish decor, served as a parallel inspiration, as a cinema in use, albeit for a different purpose.

I draw on Atwell's description of the cinema organ:

> These electric monsters were originally developed by an English-man, Hope-Jones, who went to America and basically designed the first Mighty Wurlitzer with electric action and a movable console that would loom up from the Stygian depths below the stage into view of the audience, with the organist already in full flow. This mighty monster had an average of four manuals, entailing about 200 stop keys and about 60 pistons involving as much as 100 miles of wiring. Its greatest claim was that it could imitate not only the effect of a full orchestra, but every instrument in it. Any tune could be played, any effect imitated; even drums, cymbals, castanets, sleigh-bells and whistles could be operated electrically by remote control. Their consoles were frequently... minor master-pieces of art deco design with changing light sequences.
> (ibid., 117)

The Granada, Woolwich had a pink Moorish hall of mirrors leading to the auditorium, while the Granada, Tooting had a Gothic hall of mirrors in the circle foyer. Atwell describes the latter as 'a long cloister lined throughout with cusped arches and mirrors, a journey into infinity' (131-32).

Roxy here is both star and female spectator, and there is a suggestion that the screen construct can empower as well as constrict the female gaze. Elizabeth Bowen's account of the cinema experience is perhaps representative:

> I go to the cinema ... to be distracted (or 'taken out of myself');
> I go when I don't want to think; I go when I do want to think
> and need stimulus; I go to see pretty people; I go when I want
> to see life ginned up, charged with unlikely energy; I go to
> laugh; I go to be harrowed; I ... go because I like bright lights,
> abrupt shadows, speed; I go to see America, France, Russia...
> I go because the screen is an oblong opening into the world of
> fantasy for me ... I go because I like sitting in a packed crowd in
> the dark, among hundreds riveted on the same thing.
> (from Charles Davy ed., *Footnotes to the Film*, 235; quoted by Jeffrey
> Richards, *The Age of the Dream Palace: Cinema and Society in Britain
> 1930–1939*, 23)

The reference to 'some Jack or hood' anticipates the appearance of Jack Juggler in section 48 and may recall 'starlit John' in section 39. The coffee made and not drunk is from Chantal Akerman's *Jeanne Dielman*. The legs descending the stairs are Phyllis's [i.e Barbara Stanwyck's] in *Double Indemnity*. Rita Hayworth is seen through glass splintered like a spider's web in *The Lady from Shanghai*. The 'birdlike' pose is Dietrich in a sequence in *Blonde Venus*. The juxtaposition of the locomotive wheels and the singer's face is, I think, from Lubitsch's *Monte Carlo*. The cry 'We want Claudette' is for Claudette Colbert, preferred by British audiences to her home counterparts dictated by the quota system (see Jeffrey Richards, *The Age of the Dream Palace*, 26-33; his source is an article by Ernest Dyer in *Sight and Sound*, 6, no. 24: Winter 1937–8). Marlene Dietrich scorched the soles of her feet while walking across the desert in a scene from *Morocco* (see Maria Riva, *Marlene Dietrich*, 101). 'Blocks' may suggest ruins in the sand, painterly divisions of colour and texture (as in 'set'), or simply dunes. To see is – at one level – to experience.

In Renaissance terms the whole of this section could be viewed in conjunction with the writing of Margaret Cavendish. As Kate Lilley observes:

> Cavendish repeatedly feminizes the aristocratic and chivalric trope
> (or figure) of the fair unknown. In her stories, the woman as

stranger … seduces all who encounter her, and is able to profit by the recognition of her own status as fetish. These narratives centre on the strangeness of woman, both inherent and circumstantial, and her ability to solicit and shape 'the gaze of wonder'…

The function of the blazon in [The Blazing World] subverts its customary role in the patriarchal coding of a figure of woman. Here the catalogue dwells on the account and itemization of costume, materials, colours and the emblematic accessories of power. It functions iconographically to ratify a seduction which has already occurred within the narrative – the seduction of the Blazing World by the young lady – and which is now extended to the reader.

(*The Description of a New World Called The Blazing World and Other Writings*, xvii-xxvi)

The female cinema spectator can perhaps recuperate the blazon in an equivalent way.

Jackie Stacey, discussing women's recollection of 1940s and 1950s films, comments:

Powerful female stars often play characters in punishing patriarchal narratives, where the woman is either killed off, or married, or both, but these spectators do not seem to select this aspect of their films to write about. Instead, the qualities of confidence and power are remembered as offering pleasure to female spectators in something they lack and desire.

('Feminine Fascinations: Forms of identification in star-audience relations', in *Stardom: Industry of Desire*, ed. Christine Gledhill, 152)

Stacey argues that the female spectator selects 'something which establishes a link between the star and the self based on a pre-existing part of the spectator's identity which bears a resemblance to the star' (ibid., 154).

When I heard Lorna Hutson discuss blazonry, I was struck by the way in which her dress sense subtly reinforced the argument about women deconstructing the process of 'incriminating display'. (She supplied me with a manuscript copy of the essay which later appeared in Clare Brant and Diane Purkiss ed., *Women, Texts and Histories 1575–1760*.)

Andrew Duncan

We want Claudette: substrates of *Roxy* 43

'Roxy is a kaleidoscope of female presences filtered through a male consciousness. She is a film star, an oriental or Egyptian queen, a romance novelist, a fashion model, an office worker, a sweatshop seamstress, a night-club hostess. She is a hedonist and a puritan.'

—from the original jacket text of *Roxy*

In section 43 of *Roxy* (1996, composed 1985–95) Selerie has his heroine Roxy recall a visit to the cinema whose atrium and stairwell are built in a fake Egyptian style:

> You stepped through a pylon with 'next feature' niches
> and striped papyrus columns.
> Gold lace led you down corridors
> past cobra heads and high prowed boats.
> You turned in a stair-well to see yourself
> in a double line procession,
> a foreigner nearing an urn or a platter of fruit,
> a cat-spirit reared on its hind legs
> playing a sort of flute.

Inside the auditorium,

> Lotus-flowers unfurled beside a flat crimson frame.
> A trellis with grapes edged each wall.
> A sun-disc spread wings back along the ceiling.
> Star-points joined in overlapping squares.

This is a poetic high point, with the whole building turning into a giant fetish for Colbert's Egyptian incarnation. The cinema screen intercepts only one form of beam, different screens capture different waves of the invisible. Egyptian temples were designed to capture various kinds of cosmic energy, to make the earth as serene as the heavens. Mirrors in the stairway show Roxy to herself as a part of the dazzlingly Ptolemaic décor. Cinemas were often called 'The Roxy'. We can date the visit to 1934 because the audience cry 'we want Claudette' and the Pharaonic architecture must link this to an Egyptian film, her 1934 *Cleopatra*. The poem refers to 'a bath in milk', which the audience wanted to see because they knew it would repeat the scene in the 1932 *Sign of the Cross* where Colbert, as Nero's wife Poppaea, takes her first bath in milk. With full supporting casts of slave-girls. Or do I mean maids of honour? They shout over the British supporting film, 'Quota ghosts wouldn't do – they were just/ counted out with "We want Claudette"', scorning the chance to see early performances by Basil Radford or Bernard Lee. The decor in the film on screen is continuous with the opulent and bizarrely detailed Egyptian ornament of the picture palace. *Slobbering in mud and rubies/ the idol Anubis...* the idol catches the rays in the way that black and white film captures Claudette Colbert.

We can retrieve some of the flavour of this 1934 film from reviews. So –

Devious Egyptian queen Cleopatra (Claudette Colbert) struggles to maintain her tenuous hold on her kingdom, wooing her lovers Julius Caesar (Warren William) and Marc Antony (Henry Wilcoxon) while manipulating the ongoing power struggle between the two Romans for her own nefarious ends. Director Cecil B. DeMille fills the oft-told story with lavish musical production numbers and his trademark large-scale set pieces, as well as a tongue-in-cheek attitude toward sexuality.
Initial release: 16 August 1934

An astute Amazon citizen reviewer remarks, 'There are some things that work against immersion, though. For example, apparently the clothes worn by ancient Egyptian ladies-in-waiting were a cross between the cocktail dresses and negligées of the 1930s. The writing for the speaking extras – including the venerable Florence Roberts – is exactly as awful as you would expect from the time, and so is their acting. Claudette Colbert's eyebrows are four inches long, OK, but did I notice a variation in length too?'

At a reading in about 1995 (details lost), Gavin gave out photo-copies of part of a commentary on *Roxy*, a dense mixture of handwritten text and graphics exploring labyrinthine and subterranean connections between the fetishistic and spectacular high-points which feature in the poem. A maze of connections is like a thousand trailers from films, an endless series of high points, sounds and words mysteriously lost, salvaged from some skip in Pinewood. I still have mine. A private history of the 20th century?

The links did not go towards an exit, but whirled around in some kind of vortex. Message flowed in through apertures on all sides. The art deco picture palace in *Roxy* 43 has an insane level of detail, and that is indicative for Gavin's poetry too, layer after layer of detail on every surface. In section 44, Roxy has either become a film star or perhaps is slipping into a fantasy of her own:

> You soap your breasts with asses' milk,
> fondle a baby leopard, yawning,
> lead your lover to lie inside a shell,
> make bedroom-tempests for an audience.
> Sometimes there are no lines, just a charged look.

All of these sound like moments from a De Mille film. (We return to Cleo in section 48.) *Roxy* was aimed to be the female voice, the world seen through a woman's eyes. We have to recall that this was a response to the 1980s, when the market apparently wanted 'the lyrical treatment of romantic luxury' (Thomson on Leisen) and rejected the documentary authenticity and critical showing of social problems associated with the 70s Left. He was going showbiz. No more Straub and Huillet. *Roxy* takes on the feminine voice and the analysis of popular culture. A basic question was why people took as an ideal the visible Paradise of advertisements and (related) luxury films, and not a world of transformed social and ethical relations as proposed by socialism. The poem is an inventory of glamour objects, of fantasies almost. Roxy gazing at herself in a mirrored stairwell is a comment on the specular self. The poem describes the experience so that it acquires substance and we can understand it. The bath scene was a leitmotif for De Mille, indeed it is the cinematic device most closely associated with him:

> Whatever the story of a De Mille film of the twenties, there came an obligatory halt in the plot for a lingering scene in which the heroine, sometimes the hero, washed and anointed herself in preparation for a masquerade ball or perhaps for some less public pleasure. C.B. made of the bathroom a delightful resort which undoubtedly had its effects upon bathrooms across the nation. After generations of Puritanism, it was thrilling to be told that bodily beauties were not a shame nor a weakness. American bathrooms, previously severely utilitarian, took on the gleam of marble,

tile and chrome, and the tactile luxury of great fuzzy towels and rugs. By the end of the decade, plumbing corporations, which had never mentioned their wares in public, were taking full-page ads in newspapers and magazines displaying bathroom fixtures frankly modeled on the DeMille splendor.
(*Classic Movie Favourites* website)

Colbert must have realised she was in for a swim. *Roxy* is a move out of the alternative scene, led by the idea that critique can only work by a dialogue with illusion and that it can only address illusion by bringing the credulous person on stage. Roxy, the character, was that person. British cinema is a key site where the failure is in the grain of the illusion and yet the possibility of a better society is looking back at us in fragments of every film. Fraught... bittersweet... lost to memory...We all triumph in the films that Kathleen Byron never made. Gavin began with a mastery of the substrate, collecting and watching more British films of the Thirties and Forties than anyone else. He frequented those twilight collectors' trade meetings in car parks and waste sites, the only places where you could get DVD dubs of neglected films. To return to the illusion itself:

> The art of bathing was shown as a ceremony rather than merely a sanitary duty. Undressing was not just the removing of clothes, but a progressive revelation of entrancing beauty, a study in diminishing draperies. The point was that in no stage of dress or undress need a woman look unlovely. To this end, underclothes became visions of translucent promise and nightgowns silken sensuality and invitation.
>
> After the bathroom and the bath, the bedroom was DeMille's next choice for cinematic emphasis. Here too disrobing and robing was carried on at length and in full view of the camera. The romantic glory of the bed later culminated in a film called *The Golden Bed* in 1925. DeMille's beds were things to dream about, constructed more for art, culture, lovemaking and style, than for sleep.
>
> (Quote from *DeMille, the Man And His Pictures* by Gabe Essoe and Raymond Lee, Castle Books, NY 1970)

De Mille may have had limited imagination, but with Gloria Swanson and a marble tub he could certainly seize an audience. You could swim through a score of De Mille films without even climbing out of the bath.

Roxy, as a book, proposes to remove the male narrative of events, a clean cut to sweep female concerns towards the centre. Here is another film set:

> He climbed the gantry, took aim,
> and let the camera slide down the rails,
> steel nosing into arranged corners
> of a dream – cloth creases, strands of hair, wrist-beats.
>
> She was a statue, long-throated and gowned
> with an intricate web, night-blue with trailing stars.
> She materialised out of mist, eyelids a little weary,
> striding into focus between impossible chalk marks,
> her hair back-lit for a wide vocabulary of movement.
> *(from section 38)*

The actress is being governed by the director, and inevitably *Roxy* is uttered by a male voice even while consciously making everything feminine. But didn't Hollywood work out how to speak to women (to adapt the title of Jeanine Basinger's book)? What if a poem is made of marble, tile, and chrome?

Sign of the Cross is an obnoxiously Christian film, but it is also saturated in kitsch erotica; the number of maids of honour wriggling around is simply excessive, and by some oversight their costumes are backless and virtually frontless too. According to the specialist site precode.com, 'The film was cut liberally by local censor boards, mostly focused on the more gruesome arena scenes and Colbert's bath. The reaction from across the country was wildly mixed, with some churches going in groups to see the film while others saw this as a pristine case of Hollywood excess and immorality, the lesbian dance scene drawing special ire. […] The movie was re-released in 1935 after full Code enforcement and significantly trimmed of its more salacious moments.'

A twitch of memory re-surfaces the promo video for Benny Hill's 1972 UK number 1, 'Ernie (the fastest milkman in the West)'. He offers to give Sue, his girlfriend ('she was haughty, proud and chic') her heart's desire... 'She said she'd like to bathe in milk/ He said alright sweetheart', acceding to her patrician whims. 'Would you like it pasteurised, because pasteurised is best?... Ernie, I'll be happy if it comes up to me chest.' Surely this is an anamnesis (in the terms of Outsider Art) of Colbert in *Cleopatra*, a primal scene returning to daylight and re-staging itself with whatever material is available. How is it that people could still remember a 1934 film 38 years later? This is the sink trap of the collective unconscious, where memory keeps degraded particles of light.

The set and costume designer for *Sign* was Mitchell Leisen, an architect by training who shortly thereafter became a director. A very early work, pre-Hayes Code, is *Murder at the Vanities*, (1934) which has the haunting song 'Sweet Marijuana': 'I wait alone/ here in the Mexican sunlight/ but the Mexican sunlight/ seems so lifeless and cold. // I try to find my consolation/ with a mad desperation/ that I cannot withhold...'. He made half a dozen of my favourite films but slipped somewhat and is later recorded as being a nightclub owner in Las Vegas. My guess is that he was working as an interior designer. If you look at *Sign* it is easy to imagine that the idea of opulent and ancient palaces, filled with dancing girls kicking and smiling in profusion, was welcome to the beneficial owners of Las Vegas, and that the great casinos of the 1950s were re-creations, in more or less solid form, of the sets of De Mille movies – as created by Leisen. Who did Las Vegas learn from? The style is hypertrophied, scenographic, polychrome, historicist kitsch. Roughly. To pursue time back, the sets for films like *Sign* (the original version is 1914!) were derived from Victorian history paintings – in the style of Leighton or Alma Tadema. Kitsch never wants to go home. He directed, in 1963, *Here's Las Vegas*, and in 1967, *Spree*: 'This documentary on the nightlife of Las Vegas was filmed primarily at the Topicana and Dunes Hotels'. It is a sort of Sin City exploitation feature, and judging by the trailer may have been one of the worst films ever made. Something happened to Leisen. 'See the kind of kicks showgirls want and get after hours.' So far, so Marg Helgenberger. Where *is* that can of luminol? 'Spree shows the unnatural and abnormal doings of those who can only get their kicks from doing the unusual.' Well, the Alternative poetry scene is like that in broad daylight. Seems to be halfway between *Cover Girl* and John Waters. What does someone who stood up for glamour and decadence in the 1920s do in the year of the first Velvet Underground album? Sparkle, Mitchell, sparkle.

(Topicana? I guess it was a *hot topic*.) When I interviewed Gavin, over many days, the theme which emerged seemed to be the memory of buildings. We didn't get into buildings playing back memories, viz. cinemas. Certain Egyptian temples had special sleeping rooms, for incubation (technical term), where pilgrims could sleep while expecting to see divinely sent visions (*autopsiai*). These were the original cinemas. Decades after *Roxy*, Gavin wrote about the Stoll Film studios. He took me to see the site where their hangars had stood, five minutes away from Gavin's home in Cricklewood. This was the most lavish film studio in England in around 1930. During the war, the site had been where they built aeroplanes:

> A busy site, World War One
> as the Nieuport Nighthawk
> replacing the Sopwith Snipe
> comes off the line
>
> Jump to a GB patent, 1918
> for fuselage framework,
> its cross members and gussets
> fixed without bracing
> wires and bolts
> (from 'Up from the Vault' in *Music's Duel*)

Vast brick hangars with no internal divisions and very high ceilings had proved willing to be adapted into film studios:

> Labyrinth of memory rooms,
> enamel, concrete, steel, as 'L' outspread,
> its heart a tableau bright in dim space
> pumping a dream for critics to judge

In the poem, Gavin describes two series of short features ('two-reelers') made by Stoll Films. About fifteen of these were directed by Maurice Elvey ('over 300 feature films and innumerable shorts'). He made it from silent films in 1913 (!) to teaching at the film school where Iain Sinclair studied, circa 1962. When I asked him, Gavin wrote back with a list of the twelve best Elvey films. There is no box set. Gavin fills, in so many ways, the breach between Cecil B De Mille and Oswald Stoll.

Peterjon Skelt

'A story where none exists,
one that's constantly beginning'
from 'Possession' in *Tilting Square* (1992).

Mandie Wright

Snapshots

Passing through a gate of clay to a white-painted croft.
He was the extraordinary 'older brother' of my closest friend. I so wanted
an older brother. We had occasional exciting walks together arm-in-arm
round his garden, my friend fuming at the edges relegated to her rabbits. I
was ten. He lived on high, up separate stairs, a metaphor for life, always on
a higher plane, breathing rarer air. There were occasional bursts of whirling
energy when he would launch into our room, leap onto the beds and leave.
I admired him dreadfully.

Then teenage winds blew misty; great clouds blowing – ach, the mean
old clouds…

A clearing … a hill with a mill outside the northern city walls.
He came to a house with a rose-garden that had first belonged to a
promiscuous prince and then to the Animals. He brought music and song
and sunshine. We shared guitars and he knew every detail of every song of
Bob Dylan's – authorised and bootlegged. In a hippie house with a fluid
community, open to all, he sang his own poetry; agitated as MacColl &
Seeger, tight as Bob & the Band but always free in his expression. His own
man: his own world.

An inn in the Shakespearean mid-lands. The morning after.
I wake and hear Gavin in earnest conversation. At an early morning hour,
after the party, when most of us have thoughts only for a cup of tea he is
engrossed in examination of the verse structure of Gawain and the Green
Knight before even getting out of bed. He's behind a curtain on my landing
beneath sloping beams; a setting fitting for the temptations of Gawain.
Gavin seems more ascetic; but I'm not sure.
Azimuth arrived some time ago. We love the sounds and rhythms. I admit
to only partial understanding yet the music of it speaks. MacNeice-like, if
forced to choose between sound and sense I am drawn to sound … And
there is a balance here: poetry for the eye and poetry for the ear. There are
vignettes; some so visual in their meaning, some in their form. There is
a song to the verse. My ears prick to hear animated dissection of Anglo-

Saxon riddles between Gavin and my husband, Trevor, over breakfast. *In Shoreham* has their qualities: a puzzle and a warning. I say I hear, but really, as my world is theatre, I watch; the physical language between the two writers speaking louder to me, Gavin intense and fervent. They share hats.

A theatre in a pit in a fortified tower. In the dark someone is Broken Hearted.
You're obviously someone important says the man on my right. No, simply recording notes; I work here. But on my left, Gavin is far more interesting and interested. They lean together as a spontaneous debate on John Ford, John Webster, Thomas Dekker and Thomas Middleton strikes up; the Olivier Award judge involved and fascinated by Gavin's views and observations. I am hardly surprised. Gavin lives immersed in literature. Several pages of critique arrive for me in the post in which he admires the quality of restraint in the play's language and its ease. It seems ironic that I am the one employed to speak about it when he has the superior knowledge.

A party at the head of a hill.
A whirlwind of an event; the elements dramatic along the south coast. But while Lear raged outside in the storm, the sisters and their brother celebrated warm and indulgent in the hothouse of family and friends. Come in, she said I'll give you shelter from the storm. Gavin – earnest yet giving, patient yet full of scrutiny, ironic yet open. Always twinkling with delight to see you, always kind, always sincere.

Is the scenery changing
Am I getting it wrong
Is the whole thing going backwards…

What was it you wanted?

A place of faith in the lee of a square old queen.
The same groupings. Another, sadder, celebration – of a life well lived. We congregate and share the memories, the childhood jokes. Still apparently hilarious – I can hear his dry laugh.
His critical acuity balanced with his generosity of spirit. Their hats have changed; plus c'est la même chose.

In my end is my beginning…
And the end of all our exploring

Will be to arrive where we started
And know the place for the first time.

I wish you a place where it's always safe and warm... try imagining...
We know which door you'll be knocking on.

It's been an episodic friendship but none the less valued for that. Some
people you see when you need to, not out of daily obligation.
His energy and dedication to writing is phenomenal; his work erudite and
full of nuance and reference drawn from those greats who preceded him.
It is wonderful to leave something for posterity; may his song always be
sung.
Those who know and love him will remember beyond his words; the
essence of his being, his kindly intelligence, his sensitivity, his voice.

I gotta use words when I talk to you
But here's what I was going to say...
...Nothing at all but three things.
That's all, that's all, that's all, that's all
...and when it comes to the third, this man will not be forgotten.

****

I knew all the Selerie family: Peter and Muriel and their three children
Gavin, Clare and Angela. Music was a key part of our lives. Clare and
I loved The Beatles; Gavin and Clare had spent their early childhood in
Abbey Road, just north of the recording studio; later I shared Gavin's love
of Bob Dylan and The Incredible String Band. When I lived where the M1
begins, Gavin would regale me with folk songs, like the ballad 'Barbara
Allen' and contemporary material like 'Thirsty Boots', and 'Pack Up Your
Sorrows'. He had an early interest in Roy Harper and Richard Thompson,
notable lyricists on the British scene. As a teenager he had gone to the club
[Les] Cousins in Greek Street, where Harper and others performed. I went
there too in the 1970s. Gavin was always a little ahead of me. He wrote
songs, based on romantic relationships and political issues. He set John
Donne's 'Sweetest love I do not goe', to a tune that sensitively matched the
words. This musical dimension, especially the Elizabethan air, is a major
element in his own poetry.

We shared both musical and literary interests. My London degree was weighted towards the earliest English writings: Gavin often spoke of immersion in Anglo-Saxon and Middle English literature. He said he was fortunate that his tutors, Nick Havely and Meg Twycross, had allowed him to spend so much time researching Arthurian literature at Oxford. This went way beyond Gawain and the Green Knight, though this perhaps was our favourite text. Christopher Ball, of dictionary and canal fame, had guided Gavin through the riddles from the Exeter Book, and this influence is evident in *Azimuth* (written 1972 to 1984). The power of sound in Old English has a relationship with the use of voice, rhythm, diction and syntax in his work.

We exchanged enthusiasms. He says he particularly remembers Trevor and I making a cassette of *The World of Ewan MacColl and Peggy Seeger* vols 1 & 2 for him – stuff that has never been re-released. In return he gave us a copy of Dylan's *Basement Tapes*, circulating underground at that time.

During the 1970s Gavin had done a thesis on Shakespeare, myth and the natural world at University of York. Shakespeare has always been a delight for me, leading to some years working for the RSC. We would meet when possible to see productions in Stratford and in London at the Royal Court, the Aldwych and, somewhat later, the Barbican.

Besides Shakespeare, Gavin was particularly interested in the work of Thomas Middleton, whose easy treatment of phrasing and line appealed to him, as well as themes of desire and corruption, with bizarre psychological shifts. He had seen the RSC productions of *Women Beware Women* and *The Changeling* and enthused about the interaction between Diana Quick and Emrys James in the latter play. Clearly, Gavin was excited by the proto-Gothic elements in Middleton and Webster and these may well feed into his book *Le Fanu's Ghost*. He stressed the possibilities of juxtaposing comedy with the macabre.

We also shared a devotion to modern drama, including the theatre of the absurd, enjoying work by Strindberg, Pirandello, Beckett, Howard Barker and Caryl Churchill. Gavin is a major force in a dialogue on this in the Riverside Interview volume devoted to Tom McGrath. There is analysis of Artaud, Beckett, Brecht, Sam Shepard and Gertrude Stein, as well as performance practice (from Meyerhold through to Peter Brook and Shared Experience). Connections are made between experimental theatre and jazz and this overall interest in both drama and music is reflected in the prominence of 'voice' in Gavin's work.

There are versions of riddles ('Hals is min hwit' and 'Oft ic sceal wiþ wæge winnan') from the Exeter Book, and Anglo-Saxon charms, in *Azimuth*. Another riddle ('Mec se wæta wong'), 14 lines in the original, features in *Collected Sonnets*, alongside a charm from *Bald's Leechbook*. Quite a few of Gavin's poems have a binary line structure, reflecting Anglo-Saxon practice. Kennings occur quite frequently. *Roxy* (1996) contains much reference to Early Modern literature, for instance *Dr Faustus* – brought in via the Rose Theatre controversy of the late 1980s – and writings by Margaret Cavendish. There is also a recreation of a speech from *Tamburlaine* part I ('Neural Base') in *Collected Sonnets*. The second part of *Hariot Double* involves an approximation of Renaissance English, a little modified for current consumption. 'Briny Shifts' is a rearrangement of several passages in Chapman's *Odyssey*, easing the structure of the original line. In the middle section there is a poem, 'Banker Speak', which uses the idiom of older inhabitants of the Outer Banks, North Carolina – a form close to Early Modern vernacular. 'Nightspell', near the end of the book, draws on the romance Bevis of [South]Hampton, suggesting a sixteenth century chapbook, with phrases such as 'painim londe' and 'a lemman fonde'. Earlier syntactical constructions like the multiple negatives characteristic of Middle English sometimes leak into the first (modern) part of *Hariot Double*.

This process of echoing ancient literature continues in *Collected Sonnets*, not just in the obvious places such as the sequence *Elizabethan Overhang*, but elsewhere. There is an urge to recover older usage – both words themselves and neglected meanings.

A few years back, Gavin told me he had been reading the Alliterative *Morte Arthur*, Layamon's *Brut* and *The Cloud of Unknowing* for inspiration – both thematic and linguistic. These alongside Donne's *Devotions*, which he had in John Sparrow's edition. Gavin was amused about having taken part in a campaign for the admission of undergraduates at All Souls College, where Sparrow was based, many years before. Now he was more respectful of an institution reserved for true scholars. But radicalism remained within the traditional fabric. 'Mock Saviour', responding to xenophobic and imperialist attitudes – collective narcissism – during the Brexit campaign, draws on the late Classical *History of Alexander*, mainly in the Syriac version.

Gavin's work is intellectual but it also has an approachable tone, with careful use of colloquial language. The work doesn't necessarily feel antiquarian or esoteric, because there is so often an engagement with topical issues; for example, 'Minor Concerns' (*Music's Duel*), with its ironic epigraph quoting John Major. This is a satire on the introduction of American management practice in all sectors of British education, particularly damaging to the humanities, and indeed other areas of state-supported activity. Alas, this poem now seems more relevant than ever. Again, *Hariot Double* includes poems about digital 'Cloud' storage, the Uncertainty Principle, a recent Caribbean/U.S. hurricane and the Crossrail project. I asked Gavin whether he was worried about the amount of external reference in his poetry and he said he hoped that the reader could simply take the poem as a word construct: sound texture and whatever thematic elements come through. 'Often the work has a residue of mystery, but that can be advantageous. Most of the literature I like reveals itself in layers, from *Ulysses* to Olson and W.S. Graham.' Another feature is the presence of myth and ritual which, as implied above,has a strong connection with drama. There is a lyric pulse, which beats in his blood, reflecting deep acquaintance with poetry from Wyatt to Henry Vaughan in addition to traditional song. With or without his guitar, he is still singing.

Yasmin Skelt

*Clockwise from above:
Gavin in 2008;
Gavin & Frances Presley
in 2013 and 2014.*

David Annwn

Shape-shifter / Shift-shaper:
Surrealism through and in Gavin Selerie's poetry

Snaking relentless out of rain and snow,
other seasons and stories, it thrusts
between scorching walls and spills wider
giving the strip that sustains – a country
of green and red richly black, a coming
and going moved by a muddy star to prompt
the curved lip of the lily that avenues
back to its maker's sigh

It is not only in Selerie's enthusiasm for and direct references to the work of René Magritte, Paul Delvaux, Giorgio de Chirico, Henri Michaux and Max Ernst that one finds his sense of surrealism but, also and vitally, *in* his writing's frequent subversion of usual orthographical contours, his shifting and changing of lexical and visual registers, the spooling and merging of outlines and unnerving twists of perspective.

In the lines above quoted from 'Aspic' (*Tilting Square*), it is easy to recognise this poet's beautifully fluid turning and gliding through topographical and descriptive parameters. The sliding consciousness, the carefully-shaped modulations of attention, the skewed loops and unexpected transitions and juxtapositions between different media and registers are as much part of his art as his use and subversion of sonnet forms.

The shifting focus and use of slippage are handled so deftly and unobtrusively – with so much sensual curving of thought and image – that we do not stop or need to stop, in reading, to gain interpretative purchase. That opening 'Snaking' without, initially, its subject signifier which resolves into 'it' which then 'spills wider' between 'scorching walls' despite the 'rain and snow' (a river? The Nile? a breeze? A consciousness moving the poem?) are characteristic of this poet's work; we follow, going with the words, relishing the ride, without needing any neat descriptive logic or implied continuity. Already, in this poem from a volume of 1992, ordinary distinctions are left behind. For example, is the 'country / of green and red richly black' a geographical country, or is it a state of mental synaesthesia where green and red can simultaneously be black and a 'muddy star' prompts a flower to surge back to an exhalation by the maker of this scape? Or does the scope of the poem contain all these levels at once? The 'reeds', 'desert' and 'stone triangles' might make us think (if in abstract terms) of that Egypt mentioned on the book's last page and certainly 'Snaking' might evoke Shakespeare's Cleopatra but the poem is obviously, simultaneously, a made place, an inter-penetration of perceptions and scape, a lexical flow discovering itself, a visionary current which is borne out of the interaction with (but not limited by) an actual locale.

Selerie's poetry embodies shape-shifting and the continuously morphing and creating of sinuous shifts and transitions, These transformations and flexions allow the simultaneous and successive seeing of many viewpoints. These slidings out of self are recurrent motifs in the poems, glimpsed also in oneiric dream-states as we see in 'Crack in Space'. The poem starts seemingly casually and companionably enough with:

> We were holding a house-warming party in a place
> with a passage that ran the length of the ground floor

but then:

> I fell over a crate, knocking my head
> in the dark. Something seemed to stroke my skull
> and the sutures parted, letting another self rise
> into the air.

There is something quite literally phantasmagorical about such a moment. Thinking of Selerie's Gothic faculty, there are similar spectral flights in Charles Nodier's novel *Smarra* (1821) which itself draws heavily upon E.-G. Robertson's Fantasmagorie magic lantern show. Of course, such somatic metamorphoses also occur in a surrealist novels of the 1940s. Surrealist literature, visual art and cinema have been major influences on Selerie's work at least from *Azimuth* onwards but they are, of course, also realised in the structure and image-reels of the early sonnets. It is also easy to recognise Surrealist play and un- and re-structurings of language in 'Glossolalia' in *Collected Sonnets*, 293 or 'Faded Novel: Fine Again' (*Le Fanu's Ghost*, 110-111) and 'Chipscore for Love' (*Music's Duel*, 120-22). Another example of this unpinning of everyday logic and ways of reading can be found in 'Chaocipher' (*Le Fanu's Ghost*, 145), where we are encouraged to read across and down the pages. Prose leaches into poetry and vice versa, the formal slippage and breaching of tidy parameters continuing on all fronts. Works incorporate prose poetry or, in the case of the performance text: *Strip Signals*, the prose form encompasses poetry, resolving into a dispersal of individual words at the end.

The poet's commitment to drama (he hails from a family connected with London theatres) is also notable. He evolved as a writer, watching plays that use absurd and dreamlike elements, seeing works by Artaud, Pirandello, Ionesco, Jarry and Beckett which have illogical or so-called nonsensical scenes and bizarre language, bringing subconscious feelings and experience to the fore. He is also particularly keen on Strindberg's plays, which constitute one precursor of surrealism.

Direct encounters with surrealist art are, accordingly, conspicuous and important throughout Selerie's writing and in individual contexts. For example, 'Domain of Arnheim', a *Days of '49* outtake (*CS*, p. 220), examines or re-conjures the 1949 painting by Magritte and the story by Poe that inspired it, republished in *The Centenary Poe* of the same year. Links are established here between vivid proto-surrealist elements in Poe that made his work appeal to Magritte, and the artist's habitual cross-fertilization of themes, such as the window and broken glass motifs. The poet also places Magritte's activity within a field that includes Beckett and Sartre and Magritte's painting: *The Key of Dreams* which is also referenced in section 34. The mention of glass and windows might also bring to mind the impressive achievement of Selerie's *Roxy* (1996) and its prominent mirror-motifs which are also linked to surreal cinema. In Section 4 of that book, Roxy looks in the mirror and sees two selves:

> This was her copy self in crystal,
> a finger-induced smile,
> a white blouse and a bent knee
>
> while crazed at the corner
> a raw idol
> showed up in clouds of scented dust

The flip between 'copy self', 'raw idol', the ambiguity of 'crazed' and the move to 'scented dust' is both complex and masterly, hinting at myriad different forms of crystallization, objectification and dissolution. One theoretical edge here is Lacan's essay 'The Mirror Stage', and Alain Resnais's

L'année dernière à Marienbad also provides context, perhaps the film which has affected Selerie most powerfully over the years. For this author, Resnais's concern with memory, imagination, and identity is realized or channelled particularly via the mirror image, an appropriate cinematic emblem.

Selerie is also fascinated by the ways in which Surrealist visual artists and writers challenge ways of looking and seeing are characterised in different cultural contexts. His poems on these themes subvert the essentialist ways in which female and male gaze and gazes have been enrolled, mimicked and sometimes misrepresented. 'Phantom Mannequin' (*Days of '49* outtakes) focuses on the famous Sheila Legge costume at the 1936 London Surrealist exhibition: 'a woman with a head of roses' facing 'the gallery beside a lion', right at the sculptural centre of late empire:

> the column notes a gaping hemline
> and peep-toe shoes
> your sometime object
> walks a day mark in a painter's night box

which is a wonderful way of embodying linguistically the way that Legge's 'phantom' not only brought the suppressed energies of dreams and the subconscious into daylight, but re-structured the often restrictively gendered language of visual perception. She breaks through, the poet suggests, the ways in which women have been objectified by generations of mainly male artists. Through her costume of shock and affront, Legge and the poet are also:

> ready to turn pronouns round
> will open glittering handcuffs
> in the whoroscopic record

That's a powerful moment of lexical inventiveness and confrontation. The blurring of 'whoroscopic' subverting all attempts at prior definition, either sexual stereotypes or astrological readings. This is also borne out in the poet's comment:

> With depiction of women, in all media, I have tried to give voice
> and an active nature to what is frequently objectified. Perhaps I
> mean allowing the female to come through. Ithell Colquhoun
> is one of the many female surrealist artists I admire. Carrington,

Tanning, Varo etc. 'The Mantic Stain' (*CS*, p. 214) reflects the shape and productive method of Ithell Colquhoun's *Autumnal Equinox*, inspired by the grain of an old wooden door and the artist's sense that a figure was walking out towards her. The latter two poems form a page opening, a feature I often work into the aesthetic, and the surrealist elements in Colquhoun link up with art-based poems in *Between Tongues*, my Portuguese sequence (*Collected Sonnets*, pp. 258-60), as well as other *Days of '49* texts. (Correspondence with the author)

A London-based poet for many years with international interests and affiliations, Selerie has shown great interest in probing the interest in and interpretations of Surrealism by British authors and artists. In the interview book *Into the Labyrinth*, for example the poet also describes his involvement over the years with New Apocalypse writers and different surrealist strands in British poetry of the 1940s and 50s. Initially impressed by the work of David Gascoyne, he later showed fascination with some of George Barker's weird juxtapositions, both in poems and in *The Dead Seagull*, which he read in 1967. His performance text *Strip Signals* (1985/86) also reflects such readings, as well as his taking sounds on Surrealism in continental literature. Some prose works, such as Ruthven Todd's *The Lost Traveller* and Hugh Sykes Davies's *Petron* also inspired him to find equivalent modes of perception which we find in his subsequent poetry.

The Surrealists in their work and public pronouncements also revealed an admiration of Gothic literature. Selerie illuminates such associations in 'André Breton Dreams the Walk of Charles Maturin' (*Le Fanu's Ghost*, 309) which draws strongly on Breton's and his friends' fascination with *Melmoth the Wanderer* (1820)

A little before midnight
by the café window
one comes out of a passage
(has that body a wolf's coat?)

greenish smoke wraps the hand
that writes on stained marble
the House must Fall
(it doesn't look like a plume
it looks like a dagger)

Breton's status as a great collector of Gothic novels is hinted throughout *Le Fanu*. The lycanthrope motif ('that body a wolf's coat?') occurs in Maturin's *The Albigenses*, 1824 where Paladour meets a person who claims that he has a wolf's coat consisting of 'hairs that grow inward'. Yet these details also, of course, sign towards the works of Freud and the so-called 'Wolf Man's Dream' and Breton's own leading the Surrealists' explorations of the psychiatrist's work. The lines quoted above reveal how fluently Selerie evokes shifting miasmic layers of oneiric consciousness, the Gothic and proto-Surreal co-existing and overlapping in this sleepwalk vision. One of this poet's achievements then in *Le Fanu* is that he has imaginatively re-routed the Gothic / Surrealist associations backwards and forwards through time, showing and drawing out the rich synergies and, in the context of his poem, letting these resonate together. He has also in personal conversation with myself re-iterated several times the importance of the intersection of Gothic and that which has become known as Folk Horror with Surrealism for his work.

The other notable strain, or rather, repertoire of surrealistic currents that the poet encountered early on is seen in his exploration of American avant-garde poetries. When he bought *The New American Poetry* in the spring of 1968 and later that year when he picked up Philip Lamantia's *Selected Poems* at City Lights Bookshop, these comprised a very strong surrealist influence, an impact which was felt at the time. So, rather than the kind of American poetic 'soft surrealism' employed, for example, by Robert Bly and James Wright, Selerie liked the seismic brunt and ambition of Lamantia's poetry as well as his use of lineation, the word-clusters and seismic shifts in imagery.

One could go on to draw attention to poems like 'The Ring' *Azimuth/Music's Duel*, 20-23 and 'De Luce' (*Azimuth/Music's Duel*, 35-38) influenced by acid trips and showing the strong impress of surrealism. 'Paris 1912' from *Azimuth* employs the painter, de Chirico's, work as an element in a text which deals with different existential foci. It is a love or 'relationship' poem but clearly draws on other genres and modes. The title alludes to the place and year in which de Chirico produced his most haunting, disturbing pictures, which feature objects such as a sculpture fragment, banana and train in areas which are otherwise empty or abandoned. Once, the surrealist connections and images have been noticed, they are seen to arise throughout Selerie's work. It is enough here to register a few of the broad surrealist seams which stretch through a great many of the poems, including 'Pyramid Shots' with its references to de Chirico's paintings, 'Bulldust', a poem for William Burroughs, the left column of 'Faust Variations' and 'Dyptich', all from *Days of '49*.

Additionally, this writer's mind remains receptive to new explorations of the Surrealists' wide-ranging legacies, both in his poetry and criticism. One example brings me, by way of this discussion, close to home. In his essay: 'Lines through the Lens, the Poem-films of David Annwn and Howard Munson', the poet generously focuses on the film of my poem *Jeu de Marseilles*, (2019) concerning the deck of cards created by the Surrealists: Max Ernst, André Breton and Victor Brauner amongst others, waiting to leave Europe in 1944, writing:

> Earlier in the text, the evocation of Victor Brauner's design for the psychic Hélène Smith is particularly vivid: 'her leopard flaming hair/combusting across your fingers'. Such wording is both exact as a descriptive record and ripe for visual re-translation.
> (*Junction Box* 15)

Not the least of the pleasures also associated with reading this poet's work with his depth of interest in surrealism has been to remember our many conversations about these themes. When I assisted the launch of a conference of Claude Cahun's photography in Leeds in 2014, the poet revealed his fascination in talking of her work. Our conversations held while attending the Tate Modern exhibitions 2019–20, of Dora Maar and Dorothea Tanning's visual art, also showed his deep engagement with Surrealist women artists' ways of seeing. So, I know at first hand that this writer's multidirectional interface with Surrealisms continues to expand, change and evolve.

It has been a privilege and pleasure to explore and share Gavin Selerie's wide-ranging imaginative explorations in his poetry and conversation, and moving on from that: his profound interest in Surrealism in different media. He has explored these complex cross-cultural and medial zones with great open-mindedness, humour, sensitivity and lexical inventiveness. So much of the fabric of his poetry changes our shapes of thinking. It also embodies surrealist fluidity of outlook: the shaping of lexical / imagistic shifts and transitions which take the reader into unforeseen, sometimes bizarre, always revealing and multifarious ways of seeing.

Gavin Selerie, 1969

Randolph Healy

Minoan Miniatures

(for Gavin)

Lent

Eaten transubstance is soon forgotten.

Très luisant

This clear-sky New Year's sun
this disc incised in scattered blue
from which radiant barbs enter
tender skull-mounted orbs
which next to nil assimilate but gorge
on torrents of retinted reticles
indeterminate clarity
sparking lightning traceries.

Questionnez

Milhaud asked Satie, the latter getting drenched
on his way to Montmartre,
why he wasn't using the tightly rolled umbrella clutched
under his arm. 'Are you mad!' Satie answered,
'This is far too valuable to get wet!'
After his death friends found six identical velvet suits
and dozens of umbrellas in his flat.

Du bout de la pensée

Without lacunae a ladder is just a plank.

Postulez en vous-même

Manzana in corpore sano.
An apple a day keeps the doctor away.

Pas à pas

Static erased your nascent song.
O opaline world abrupted, for what?
No reason.
Ghosts orbit full tilt in vacuo.

Under, a furnace is frozen.
Nadir, I implore you
Send grief, hurt, rage.
Unlevel this spirit
Necrotically making do.
Grace it with agonies to feed.

Sur la langue

Sinuous, sliding source
of silly and celestial,
darting, lashing, tale-teller,
print unique as those digital,
caruncles secrete,
silver devils,
Jas. 3: unruly evil, sink of iniquity,
slitherer, roaming such little labyrinth,
seeker of fragments,
testing each crevice,
ticklish sensories throng thy terminus
on which little skillet salt doth sizzle,
saluti.

Lesley Newland

It's many years ago now that Gavin first introduced David and myself to 'The Queen's Larder'. I didn't know the pub before which is surprising because it's round the corner from Queen's Square where I took some of my exams. As we're aware, medical students from St Bartholomew's Hospital know most of the pubs in London.

'The Queen's Larder' is close to the Bedford Hotel where we often stay when in London with the Marchmont Association's blue tile for Emmeline Pankhurst and her daughters Christabel and Sylvia at 8 Russell Square close by, a Feminist statement dear to my heart. There's also the close proximity of the British Museum and the Queen Square Gardens.

We have of course met Gavin in many other places but perhaps the best is the snug, cottage-like feel of 'The Queen's Larder', the basement of which, so tradition suggests, was used by Queen Charlotte to stock food for her ailing husband, the so-called 'Mad King' George.

Our visits to this venue after a meal at a nearby restaurant bring back some of the most vivid and warm memories: the lively, intelligent bar-staff, the clientele from round the world and the precarious climb to the Ladies loo. Above the bar in the pub is a collection of some very scary clowns. Gavin is always as interested in the almost life-sized clowns perched on the shelf above the bar as I am. Wherever did these puppets or models come from? They are silent watchers, bizarre and colourful. They are also a fitting accompaniment to Gavin's fascinating stories, theatrical gestures, circuitous interjections, learned verbal footnotes and rumbustious laughter. We always have such wonderful times there together with our dear friend!

On one occasion in this pub in 2018, one of the bar-staff offered to take our photo and, just as if one of the Clowns was manipulating space, because of a trick of perspective, Gavin seems to have grown the most enormous arm with a huge hand! It is a moment worthy of visual theatre. Somehow the ornate curtains, lamps, mirrors and white flowers all contribute to the illusion and Gavin looks amused and serene, as if already aware of the joke the photo would create and at home with red wine, in the ancestral Larder between David and myself. Cheers!

Lesley Newland, Gavin Selerie and David Annwn, 20 March, 2018

Ian Brinton

Three translations of Francis Ponge
for Gavin Selerie

Bread

Above all the surface of bread is wonderful as it offers a panoramic impression: it is as if you feel within your grasp the Alps, the Taurus or the Cordillera of the Andes.

An amorphous mass, on the point of belching out, was slid for our sake into a star-shaped oven in which, as it hardened out, there formed valleys, crests, both highs and lows… and from here the thin flagstones, those carefully laid-out plans upon which the light lays its heat to bed – with little regard for the vulgar flab beneath.

The cold slack subsoil, the loaf's soft crumb, possesses a tissue not dissimilar to a sponge: both leaf and flower are joined at all points like Siamese twins. As the bread stales the flowers wilt and wither: they loosen themselves from each other and the mass crumbles…

Let's leave it there: a mouthful of bread is more to do with food than being a symbol of respect.

Fire

Fire is just in a class of its own: to begin with all its shoots seem to make headway for each other…

(You can't begin to compare the march of a fire with beasts on the move: they have to leave one place in order to arrive at another; fire shifts like an amoeba as well as like a giraffe, a leaping neck and creeping feet)…

And then, whilst the burnt masses collapse fire's fumes are let free like an explosion of butterflies.

The Seasonal Cycle

Fed up with being confined throughout the winter, trees all at once start to feel that they've been had. They cannot put up with it any longer and so now let their words out: a flood, a vomiting of greenness. They try to build up a complete foliation of language. As if! That will take place as it may and indeed does. There's nothing random about foliation…They release, well at least they think they do, loads of language and twigs too from which to hang words: our trunks, or so they imagine, are there to take over the world. They try to conceal themselves by hiding one behind the other. Although they think that they can say it all by covering the earth with a variety of different tongues, they actually only blurt out *'TREES'*. They can't even hang on to the birds which disappear out of them even as they are clapping themselves for producing such an unusual array of flowers. Always the same leaf, always the same manner of unfurling; the same number, with each one looking the same as its neighbour, appearing in symmetrical suspense. Fancy another leaf? – It's the same! How about another? Same again! The only thing to make them pause might be the phrase 'You can't see the wood for the trees.' A moment of exhaustion, a shift of stance. 'Let all of it turn yellow and then fall. Bring on some withering quiet: *AUTUMN'*.

David Hackbridge Johnson

Some Riffs on Gavin Selerie

Lying in a cupboard, loved albeit now un-played, is a Selmer Rancher guitar of late 1960s vintage, belonging to poet Gavin Selerie. It has the characteristic batwing-shaped scratch plate of the model and is in pretty good nick save for a missing D string. With a tune-up and a polish it is ready for a gig. The guitar was in use up until 15 years ago and seeing it coming out of its case might trigger the memory of its sound and the feel of its vibrations under the fingertips – the guitar being perhaps the most tactile of all instruments, the sound seeming to pass from hand to hand, the fingers striving to extend the orbit of a note or chord that always threatens to fade before its expressive bloom can tell. Looking around the North London flat of the poet, one expects to see books – and there they are, neatly yet somehow precipitously arrayed in cliff faces of bound texts – yet in between the shelves are slimmer holdings of CDs, both commercial and home recorded. Here are a thousand guitars preserved on silver discs. The range is hard to take in since in addition to the expected names of established artists across many genres, are the obscure, the forgotten, the barely rescuable, even the irredeemable. And the guitar is often the instrument of choice as a plethora of blues bands, territory bands, jug bands, folk bands and even the lonely guitarist waiting, perhaps unwisely, at the crossroads, dominate the CD towers. Like looking at a guitar, looking at the spine of a CD can conjure the memory of its sounds: Skip James picking out a rolling bass line for his piercing tenor voice to ride in *Hard Time Killin' Floor Blues*, Peg Leg Howell hanging his *glissando* vocal swoops on chiming gospel-like chords in *Tishamingo Blues*, Robin Williamson threading a Celtic knot for his keening voice to unravel in The Incredible String Band's *October Song*. Another tower, pressed between bulging shelves of Beat poets and Coleridge's *Notebooks*, is filled with the names of those trail blazers of contemporary British jazz active from the 1960s onwards, among them, Derek Bailey, Elton Dean, Michael Garrick, Jim Dvorak, Norma Winstone, Keith Tippett, and Louis Moholo. The CD spines here jolt into the mind's ear actual live performances featuring these musicians that in all likelihood we both attended – when I first met Gavin Selerie it was this unbeknownst shared listening that we tried to establish; on which gig did Derek Bailey sit in with the Cecil Taylor Trio?, who was on bass for that Elton Dean Vortex gig in late 1990? And, did Gavin even hear *me* in my drumming days when I was playing for Harry Beckett and Alison Raynor? Probably not, for I was fleeting, and then fell into writing symphonies.

A cursory glance at Gavin Selerie's bibliography will flag up immediately his deep affinity to music; two large collections announce this in their very titles: *Music's Duel* (Shearsman, 2009) and perhaps more obliquely *Hariot Double* (Five Seasons Press, 2016). And although *Roxy* (West House Books, 1996) has a purview beyond music, its title suggests Bryan Ferry's work with the band Roxy Music as one of the book's starting points. The title of *Hariot Double* is a multi-level pun; the spelling of Hariot refers to the astronomer and ethnographer Thomas Hariot (c.1560–1621) yet if both the 'r' and the 't' in his name are doubled we get Harriott, as in the Jamaican saxophonist Joe Harriott (1928-1973). Mention might be made of the use of the word 'double' as it relates to works that employ the term to mean 'variation', such as those by J. S. Bach; the four movements of his *Partita in B minor* BWV 1002 for solo violin, all of which have an initial statement followed by its double, being well-known examples. We might conclude that Harriott is a 'double' of Hariot as he traverses musical orbits in response to those studied by the astronomer – a kind of jazz *doppelgänger* if you will. The book's protagonists engage in a 'call and response' pattern in both musical and astronomical shapes; my own copy has the following inscription from the poet: 'to David and Xiaowei a double history across centuries'. Hariot the astronomer is a figure known perhaps only to renaissance specialists; Harriott the saxophonist is closer to us in time but his trajectory was as that of a blazing comet that lit up the sky only to depart leaving a vapour trail of wailing blues notes and double-time runs. Double again. All this elliptical fancy might have led to an arcane disquisition in jazz metaphysics combined with historical snapshots, yet Selerie is able to root his poems in experience of actual performances. The poet is at a gig at the Oxford Union on 18th October, 1966 and this engenders an exhortation, from musician to audience or visa versa: 'Jump, jump the divide, blow / through stone'[1] – as if a saxophonist is capable of both leaping through time and space, and driving through matter. This already gives a tight fist of information to unravel, yet Selerie also wants the set list in the poem so we can know the melodies and chord sequences that will provide springboards for these Einsteinian ventures: *They Can't Stay Away*, *Perdido*, an unnamed Blues

---

[1] 'Horn for Hire', from *Hariot Double*, p. 108. I must mention here the striking graphic contributions to the book of fellow poet Alan Halsey.

in C, *Here's That Rainy Day, Love for Sale, Jackie-ing, St. Thomas* and *East of the Sun*. Each tune gets a stanza (or we might say a jazz chorus) where Selerie combines musical points of analysis ('Latin on the outsides / and steady for the middle' … 'a phrase displaced' … 'a calypso bounce') with wry asides of emotional debris: '*Here's That Rainy* (how love becomes)' … '*East of the Sun* (keep it that way)'.[2] Such is the connectivity between note and word that Selerie is able to 'hear' the speech of the saxophonist's utterances: 'Twist the notes around, / a little growl, almost a word.' All this adds up to a vivid recollection of what was no doubt an exciting gig. But an astronomical ghost is sitting in a corner; there are hints in the poem: 'horizon', 'annex the planets', 'the tonic always to dip / and climb back'[3] – this last fragment suggestive of both departure and return to a key centre and the rising and falling of heavenly objects in the sky, a thought that brings Kepler's *Harmonices Mundi* of 1619 into view; we know that Hariot was corresponding with Kepler via an intermediary, so perhaps they discussed the music of the spheres. In any case, Harriott jumps through the centuries to find Hariot tapping his foot in the snug bar of an alehouse. In this one poem alone it can be seen that Selerie is keeping many things aloft in a kind of poetic orrery; further explorations of both *Hariot Double* and his other musically inspired work would reveal much. That musical terminology peppers Selerie's texts is easy to discover: out-take, track, consort, canon, feedback, strain, saraband – once you spot these references you can't stop seeing them.

Beginning and ending with the guitar. One aspect of Selerie's love of the instrument is reflected in his work inspired by Bob Dylan. There are several pen and ink drawings of Dylan, two of which feature the singer with his guitar, that Selerie made for his pamphlet *Vitagraph* (Binnacle Press, 2001); they remind us that before turning to writing, Selerie had considered art as his *métier*. The title of the pamphlet is presented as one word on the title page, which might suggest the old Brooklyn-based picture studio, but as Vita Graph on the front cover; I think the reader is encouraged to read this as 'Life Network'. Such a network begins the book; an extended riff on Dylan song titles and lyric fragments put through a Selerie filter process. In light of the astro-jazz of *Hariot Double*, one can't help noticing 'laid bright on double'.[4] *Vitagraph* concludes with a perceptive essay about Dylan which covers Selerie's first hearings and his analysis of repertoire and recording

---

[2] Ibid. pp. 108-109.
[3] Ibid. pp. 108-109.
[4] *Vitagraph*, p. 7.

techniques; the essay is of interest to social and musical historians. Selerie has written on Dylan almost every year for various publications; it is hoped an opportunity will arise to collect these essays. What was it about Dylan that captured the interest of so many? The early Dylan performances, where he is effectively a one-man trio of voice, guitar and harmonica, encapsulate a fusion of blues, folk and poetry that draws from all those traditions to create a style that felt new to audiences of the 1960s. Selerie describes his early discovery of Leadbelly (about whom he wrote in *Days of '49*)[5] and Dylan, as giving access to 'a kind of secret knowledge'[6] not at all in keeping with the ethos of the traditional boarding school he was attending at the time. Some of Selerie's blues lyrics or sonnets, of which there are a number, could even be imagined as being sung by Dylan, especially 'Snatch It Back Blues' with its almost drawling rhythm: 'Cheers some hooted, the stony heart / to shake and brace a lolling dream / vented, against all seeming habit / of me-first you-win tenders'[7] – imagine the harmonica rasp, here, and the extra rip in the guitar chords. Or am I just rhyming 'lolling dream' with 'rolling stone'? Dylan, like his blues and folk predecessors, is more than just an entertainer; like many such artists without his seeming world appeal, Dylan also appears to have discoverable messages. This is particularly true up until 1964 when he claimed he was no longer interested in politics or at least writing protest songs. Music and message in Selerie would be a whole new topic beyond the scope of what is essayed here, but like so much of the poet's work that gives up new meanings on each new reading, it is a topic worthy of exploration.

The foregoing is but a sketch of musical interactions to be found in the poetry of Gavin Selerie; a full exegesis of this theme would take up too much solo space; as Miles Davis said to John Coltrane when the latter didn't know when to end a solo: 'just take the horn out of your mouth.'

---

[5] Alan Halsey & Gavin Selerie, *Days of '49*, West House Books, 1999,

[6] 'Gavin Selerie interview, part 2', *Angel Exhaust*, November 2011. http://angelexhaust.blogspot.com/2014/03/azimuth-and-digression-gavin-selerie.html?m=0 (last accessed 11.x.2022).

[7] *Music's Duel*, p. 294.

Gavin Selerie

Long Haul Voices: the Book Length Poem

This is a record of my engagement with the long poem form, taking note of its nature and development from the classical epic onwards. The term varies in definition. Is length the key factor or is it rather a narrative or philosophical breadth and complexity? Can Eliot's *The Waste Land*, described by him as 'a long poem' in May 1921 but subsequently cut to nearly half its length by Pound, be classed in this category? The notes Eliot supplied at a late stage were done to fill out the text for book publication. Bunting's *Briggflatts*, another example of severe contraction but this time by the author, was issued as a book, albeit a thin one, by Fulcrum Press. These works consist respectively of 433 and 700 lines. Can these be at all comparable with *Paradise Lost, Don Juan* or H.D.'s *Helen in Egypt*? In scope perhaps but not in structure and size.

Much of what we are is formed early in life. One of the few activities I enjoyed at boarding school was running long distance through what was then the largely unspoilt countryside of the Hertford/Hoddesdon/Ware triangle, and as many of my friends will testify I have an unusual tolerance for long stories and sequences. As a child I heard my father recite sections from *Idylls of the King*, though his favourite, 'The Passing of Arthur' had existed as a standalone lyric ('Morte d'Arthur'). My paternal grandparents' home was full of Victoriana, with Pre-Raphaelite paintings and books such as Tennyson's in gilt bindings. I think I imbibed something of this exoticism and in the case of Tennyson the Arthurian epic fed into my experience of Cornish and Breton landscape on family holidays. Later I studied parts of Wordsworth's *The Prelude*, Coleridge's *Rime of the Ancient Mariner* and Keats's *Hyperion* poems for A Level. These examples of Romantic epic – if the term is applicable to such diverse works – involve a sustained progressive narrative. Within the longer stretch I was drawn to Wordsworth's concept of 'spots of time': incidents grounded in space that come to have epiphanic significance.

I spent what would now be termed a gap year (actually eight months) in the USA and Canada. Here, early in 1968, I bought Donald Allen's anthology *The New American Poetry* which, despite my previous knowledge of some of the poets, proved a revelation. The most significant fallout was exposure to the work of poets associated with Black Mountain College, which developed further on my return to Britain. I also acquired *Confucius to Cummings*, edited by Ezra Pound and Marcella Spann. Among other things, this directed me to Gavin Douglas's version of the *Aeneid*, which I subsequently accessed more fully in *The Poetical Works* (1874). Elsewhere, Pound described the *Eneados* as 'better than the original, as Douglas had heard the sea.'[1] The passages which deal with the elements, including the time or season section-openings, proved a lasting pointer.

For the Middle English part of my first degree I focused particularly on Arthurian romance, with attention to ritual and the supernatural. Hence, in addition to *Gawain*, *Troilus and Criseyde* and other obvious texts, I read a lot of verse romances, including the alliterative *Morte Arthure*. As part of Anglo-Saxon studies, I got immersed in the epic *Beowulf*, fascinated by its jugglings with time, which disrupt the sequential process. I was also intrigued by the layering of Christian and pagan elements. Coverage of early modern literature embraced *The Faerie Queene*, which I read, as if it were a novel, in the Oxford Parks. I was attracted by Spenser's tangled forests and wandering, which are literalized in the poem's digressive and incomplete structure. The knights never finish their quests and the Mutability Cantos at the (provisional) end suggest a contingent reality. Any narrative or philosophical scheme seems less significant than the thread of imagery and the pictorial detail at a local level. I was struck by the way in which abstract ideas are given concrete force, as with the turret of the mind (II.ix) or the mirror that enables Britomart to see a far-off Artegall (III.ii).

My experience of Renaissance drama, both through the texts and in performance, was also influential. I kept coming back to the notion of 'Negative Capability' in Shakespeare,[2] which I interpreted as the ability to inhabit different and opposing forms, whether persons or ideas. That is, resisting the urge to impose an attitude or judgment. When I came to read Olson's essays I found that he too saw Keats's statement as a guide to letting contradictions co-exist. In *The Special View of History* Olson links this with Heraclitus's theory of flux and Heisenberg's Uncertainty Principle, with emphasis on existence as process.[3]

---

[1] Ezra Pound, *Literary Essays* (Faber & Faber, 1954), 35

[2] H.E. Rollins (ed), *The Letters of John Keats* (Cambridge University Press, 1958), I, 193.

[3] Charles Olson, *The Special View of History* (Oyez, 1970), 41-42

The crucial eighteenth-century poetic text I studied was Pope's *Dunciad*, which enacts a 'motley mixture' of themes and situations, with a self-reflexive concern for the printed word. Later, in the early 1990s, I acquired the quarto Variorum (1729) in facsimile, which provided a crucial inspiration for my book length poem *Roxy*. As an undergraduate I also read parts of Byron's *Don Juan*, but it was only in the 1980s that I came to read the whole thing, again an influence on *Roxy*. I see it as having more fluidity of transition than *The Dunciad*, with spontaneity of the moment and an easier take on the poetic line, but clearly the two works have elements in common. The Romantic context brings me to Blake's prophetic poems, particularly *The Four Zoas*. What especially drew my attention was the way in which Blake combines commentary on contemporary events with a larger sense of myth and archetype. An example is the treatment of metal work as slavery under Urizen's war machine, yet fulfilling in a time of peace. Besides its tracing of political events of the period 1797–1807, the poem sets up a layered history of the personality with all its twists and turns; this is accentuated by the long period of composition, allowing different emphases and departures, but also perhaps preventing completion of the work. I find it all the more interesting for this fractured process.

During this period I also absorbed classical epic in modern translations, for instance C. Day Lewis's rendering of the *Aeneid* and Fitzgerald's *Odyssey*. Only in the decade that followed did I read Chapman's Homer, Golding's version of the *Metamorphoses* and Stanyhurst's Virgil, all remarkable for their linguistic texture. Pound championed Golding's Ovid[4] and it is clear that the Latin poet's weave of motifs, as well as the whole business of turned shapes, is an influence on the *Cantos*, despite the modernist omission of connectives. I saw the continuing relevance of this kaleidoscope of tales with dramatized moments of revelation. Later still, I encountered Derek Walcott's *Omeros*, an ambitious cultural transposition which nevertheless lacks the rhythmic acuteness and improvisational drive of his Caribbean contemporaries Brathwaite and Glissant.

I went to lectures on modernist literature but most of my reading was the result of personal enthusiasms. I bought Pound's *Cantos* in 1969 and saw immediately how this connected with Olson's later practice. I was impressed by the sinuous mode of arguing, the sharpness of imagery and the melodic flow. Themes, figures and events were interwoven in a way that seemed true to mental experience. Thus Canto XVI – one of the great First World War poems – registers the toll of combat, focusing on lives lost

---

[4] See *Literary Essays*, passim.

or wrecked, each with a personal cadence. But this is performed within a long historical reach, whereby, for instance, the visionary Blake – a sort of hell guide – is trapped within the system he opposes. The opening of *Three Cantos*, later adapted as the start to Canto II, shows how Pound envisaged his approach to epic, rejecting what came before yet re-angling usable technique. Browning's 'bag of tricks' in *Sordello* could be relevant if 'the modern world/Needs such a rag-bag to stuff all its thought in'.[5]

Alongside Pound and Olson, I read Roy Fisher's 'assemblage' *City*, parts of the sequence *Passages* in Robert Duncan's *Bending the Bow*, and Bunting's *Briggflatts*, the latter particularly interesting for its musical structure. A few years later I discovered Carlos Williams's *Paterson*, which mixes prose and verse, supposedly inspired by Ford Madox Ford's call for poetry to reflect the 'normal life of the street'.[6] The importation of a documentary-style transcription of 'reality' is a useful resource, though some might feel the material is insufficiently mediated. Another example of mixed form is David Jones's *Anathemata*, which again switches between verse and prose in the main text but also has an extensive footnote apparatus. Jones's preface cites Nennius's statement, 'I have made a heap of all that I could find',[7] and it is possible to see the work as a kind of memory atlas, with close attention to place. A more zany, contemporary approach is the radio-like splay of voices in Edward Dorn's *Gunslinger*.

I seem naturally drawn to structures which involve cumulative and twisting elements. The modernist long poem offers an escape from closure while still allowing progression. There is often a displacement of temporality. This is true of the *Cantos*, despite Pound's background sense of an epic that moves from the Dark Forest, through the Purgatory of human error, to a state of Light. In Olson's *Maximus* the chronicle of the town's history is mediated or complicated by mytho-cosmology and the personal, daily experience of the poet. Such a structure involves layered perception.

* * * * *

---

[5] Ronald Bush, *The Genesis of Ezra Pound's Cantos* (Princeton University Press, 1976), 53

[6] James Guimond, *The Art of William Carlos Williams* (University of Illinois Press, 1968), 155; Ford Madox Ford, *Mightier Than the Sword* (Allen & Unwin, 1938), 260-61

[7] David Jones, *The Anathemata* (Faber & Faber, 1952), 9

Since starting seriously in 1972 I've written several books that, in different ways, constitute 'long poems'. The first was *Azimuth* (1984), which combines verse and prose in atomized but related units. Like Zukofsky's *'A'*, at one level the progress is autobiographical, but it also traces broader cultural shifts, contemporary and historical. There is a strong focus on landscape, as plotted in print and walked or driven through in the live moment. I aspire to comprehend the vast, and attend to the minute, as Johnson said of James Thomson.[8] But my procedure is opposite to that example of practice. Modes of navigation are implied in the title *Azimuth*, yet the progress is diffuse and oblique, driven by chance rather than a master scheme. This method reflects my experience of free form jazz and also an awareness of noise distribution, as practised by Pink Floyd, who used an 'azimuth projector' to release layers of sound around a performance venue. Olson was an inspiration here, showing how you could utilise diverse materials within a longer text: primitive mythology, Jungian dreams, historical records, scientific theory alongside personal observation – a sliding reality that combines oral discourse with more formal analysis, their exact status open in the final text. Andrew Duncan has observed that the poem 'has a centre in a dozen different places.'[9] Granted that fluidity, there is a mesh of recurrent motifs and, in what has become my usual practice, a chain of paired poems and mini-sequences. These are arranged within and across seven main sections. From an early age I have been keenly aware of the spatial qualities of words and I treat the text on the page as a kind of picture. Sound, naturally, is part of this deployment: the charting of a score. The layout of text in *Azimuth* and later works is influenced by the Constructivist concepts of *faktura* (the texture or material properties of an object) and *tektonika* (spatial presence). A pattern poem such as 'Wormenhert' (40) reflects awareness of a form that runs back through early modern to classical literature, and such practice was aided by the book being printed from my electric typewriter script, including paste-ups.

When I was about two-thirds of the way through writing the book, I became aware of Allen Fisher's *Place* sequence,[10] reading it in the original editions and hearing it voiced as the work developed. It transpired that Fisher and I had been using some common sources such as Nicholas

---

[8] Samuel Johnson, *Lives of the English Poets* (Oxford University Press, 1952), II, 358

[9] *Into the Labyrinth*, http://www.argotistonline.co.uk/INTO%20THE%20LAB YRINTH.pdf : 13

[10] Allen Fisher, *Place* (Reality Street, 2005)

Barton's *The Lost Rivers of London* and John Michell's *View Over Atlantis*. My take on things is, nevertheless, different, with a strong focus on romantic relationships. The textual history of *Azimuth* is complicated, with outtakes appearing in *Puzzle Canon* (1986) and subsequent books. When a *Selected Poems* was planned in the early 1990s I revised certain pieces, some of which appear in *Music's Duel* (2009). These are still my preferred versions.

For the next decade I worked on *Roxy* (1996), which consists of 52 sections with an end-note. The poem concerns style in its various manifestations, from fashion in dress to modes of speech, and its dialectical process draws equally on esoteric and popular culture and ranges from the present back through the ages. The book could be described as a biography of form. It is partly a response to Elizabeth Wilson's *Adorned in Dreams*,[11] which had just come out, and to volume I of Braudel's *Civilization and Capitalism*,[12] where the significance of fashion is examined. Each argues that style of attire is an indication of deep phenomena rather than a surface element. Wilson defends consumer culture against the charge that it is nothing more than 'false consciousness'. She sees fashion as reflecting 'the ambivalence of the fissured culture of modernity'. A vehicle for fantasy, involving both subjugation and liberation, it is a means of complex expression. These ideas fed into what I already knew about the Art-Nature debate in the Renaissance, the Aesthetic Movement in the nineteenth century, and Wyndham Lewis's championing of the outside of things.[13] Londoners probably have a heightened sense of 'deep' surface. *Roxy* grows out of the everyday experience of living in Ladbroke Grove: observing the street styles of Portobello Road, sitting in the Electric Cinema, and so on. Wider phenomena intersect with this: the King's Cross fire (1987), the burning of *The Satanic Verses* in Bradford and the exposure of the Rose Theatre site (both 1989) are among the contemporary events referenced. A spectrum of current literary activity also figures here.

The title suggests glamour, eroticism and enigma, including wiles in pursuit of power, and the poem subjects this to interrogation. The various female presences in the poem are filtered through a male consciousness, yet forms of destabilization are used to signal the constructedness of the images. I drew on feminist film theory to reverse or qualify stereotypes. My use of different voices folding in and out of one another, fragmenting

---

[11] Elizabeth Wilson, *Adorned in Dreams: Fashion and Modernity* (Virago, 1985)
[12] Fernand Braudel, *Civilization and Capitalism 15th–18th Century*, vol I: *The Structures of Everyday Life* (Collins, 1981)
[13] See particularly *Blasting & Bombardiering* (Eyre & Spottiswoode, 1937), 9

and coalescing, makes the poem close to drama – at least that type of text for performance in which the subjective 'I' is unstable. One of the epigraphs in *Azimuth* is Godard's line from *Vivre sa Vie*: 'Error is necessary to truth' (293). Here a shrill rhetoric is challenged and contained by a warmer tone, which shifts again into something else. There is no single overarching voice, although at times an embodied authorial voice is privileged. Assertion is undercut by assertion or by internal inconsistency, so that the text is in argument with itself – which is not to deny its radical thrust. *Roxy* describes, enacts and counters the Thatcher-Murdoch era: a forbidding sheen summed up by the image of a publisher's tower at the end of section 18:

> There's further thinking to do, surely
> from an armchair or a leather-topped desk:
> the product is pulp, barbered up.
> the product is congealed labour,
> the product is an emblem of rights –
> a non-discernible future –
> bought and sold from a skyish bookcase
> barred to the real maker.

In the broadest sense the poem concerns the politics of style. It has more apparent consistency than my other long poems because all the text is aligned at the left margin, but within that scheme there is variation, as in the length of sections, pairing of pieces and incorporation of song and dialogue. Given its theme, the look of the book was particularly important. A bromide printout of my computer-set text was used at source to give the lettering a fuller body.

Le Fanu's Ghost, written in 2001–2006, is an exploration of interfamilial and literary relationships, mainly Irish. Formally, it reflects my interest in marginalia procedures, which have a special pertinence to Gothic, with its hidden corners, splintered selves and instability of narrative or viewpoint. The main text in six sections is bookended by a prologue and a personalia, providing further context for an intricate weave of material, often playful. As with *Roxy*, the book was not written in sequence from beginning to end; rather, texts were laid out across the whole span in such a way that further material could be accommodated. Once laid in position the pieces were rarely moved from their ongoing structural track; however, they acquired further definition through the slotting in of new material. This was appropriate to my continual discovery of related features. Accretions to a basic thread resulted in a layered and winding pattern, like an illuminated manuscript and Celtic tracery. I was able to develop a sliding frame of reference, with smaller things contained within and spreading outside the main detail. Thus 'Chinks in the Word Machine' (313), which deals with genetic make-up and the recording and transmission of experience, has five component parts that relate to each other and to the book as a whole. 'Glass Master' (78-82) uses imagery of CD manufacture and operation to explore Irish history, including the Troubles:

> spin for tonight only
> fast aflutter slowed
> the cry that cries to cry
> one heart one tongue one ground
> when the fork is driven deep
> …
>
> > open coat hands on head
> > what's the name where
> > you going
>
> cake the walls with a kind of mud
> (why say helpless) as the blatant beast
> in a key-cold embrace
> blankets one stark hide

Shape poems such as 'Mizmaze Mizzard' (129) which summons Swift and Vanessa through *Finnegans Wake*, contribute to the active intermedial set-up, produced through a mixture of control and accident. Alan Halsey, who had supplied section emblems for *Azimuth*, created a frontispiece and illustrations to begin each section. The process was collaborative in that I provided relevant source images, along with some notes on routes and focus. His graphics reflect key motifs such as the portrait or mirror on the wall, a crumbling mansion, a theatre auditorium and a gaming table. He was also responsive to my mention of 'framing possibilities', creating pictures-within-pictures.

Hariot Double, written in 2009–2016, attempts to combine the intensity of the short lyric with a more sustained ruminative thread. From childhood on I've been fascinated by Elizabethan voyage literature and I'm also a devotee of free form jazz, including British material. Musing on the name 'Harriot' in its various spellings, I was drawn to see parallels between these distant cultural contexts. The poem that emerged is a dual narrative, with the life of saxophonist Joe Harriott moving from birth to death and the life of scientist-adventurer Thomas Hariot moving from death to birth, so that the book enacts a cycle. In between there is a long sequence which deals with contemporary events, that is, the period of the writing of this work. Here, for instance, Hurricane Irene on the Outer Banks is juxtaposed with Crossrail tunnelling in London, 'Cloud' storage and the fallout of the 2008 financial crash. The trajectories of the two Hariots – including the jazz player's Jamaican origins and the Elizabethan's ventures in Virginia and Ireland – led me to consideration of empire and colonization. Hence civilization versus barbarism is a major concern, with the regular scale subjected to interrogation and inversion.

In 'Stereo-isomeric' (215) Joe addresses Thomas as a kindred but strange self:

Your gown is my skin. This sunburn
you purchased over the main
shot convulsive through foam
to find grapes and cedars. I followed back
to make good, stayed to plant in reverse
a sort of twisted wire.

The title refers to a situation where you have molecules that contain the same number and kinds of atoms but differ from each other in spatial orientation. At the risk of stating the obvious, Thomas Hariot's preferred dress was a black gown; his journey to the New World involved documentation of natural resources; and Joe Harriott's development of free jazz in London met with some resistance.

As with my previous long poems, this book is a mosaic, built up in layers. Motifs emerge, fade and re-emerge in variations. As well as parallels across the three sections, there are mini-sequences and companion pieces placed adjacent to one another. On page 350 'Chap-venture' (about the construction of toy boats) makes passing reference to the chap-book romance *Sir Bevis*, and three pages later the poem 'Nightspell' provides a condensed version of that story. References to the Bank of England, under which Thomas Hariot was buried when part of the site was a church, tie in with Joe Harriott's financial struggles and the economics of imperialism.

I've walked or sailed on much of the territory described in the book, liaising with experts and chatting casually to people along the way. It is important to stress the latter because significant knowledge emerged from chance encounters.

Documentary material is woven in with the imaginative. Sometimes the documentary-type stuff is taken over fairly straight (but often telescoped and collaged); at other times the text is 'new'. For instance, 'Excursive' (259-60) – evoking Queen Anna's visit to Syon House – may look as if it is based on a journal reminiscence or letter, but it's entirely imagined, apart from a couple of phrases from correspondence and an anecdote. 'Briny Shifts' (236) is a rearrangement of several passages dealing with Odysseus's descent to the underworld (see *The Odyssey*, books 10 and 11). I adapt Chapman's phrasing, for the most part avoiding end-rhyme, and a comparison will show the extent of recreation as opposed to mere imitation. 'Walk out from where…' does not sound like the Renaissance poet. Chapman allowed Thomas Hariot to see his translation in process, so here the Homeric matter extends to other pieces such as 'Calypso Gloriana' (151-53). It was a linguistic challenge to incorporate some patois in Section One and to re-create early modern idiom in Section Two. By a sort of cubist technique the voice mode oscillates between inside consciousness and outside – a spread that involves different people as well as the selves of an individual, not always demarcated.

The double motif involves split perspectives, as well as overlay. Narrative is destabilized through shifts into other times and spheres. The whole of the Intermean section is a kind of digression but with relevance to the two main parts. You could say I've put marginalia at the centre. The book has many shape poems, such as 'Kinsey Rite' (35) which suggests a lamp or heart, and 'Space Monkey' (95) in the form of a rocket. This aspect is extended via Alan Halsey's graphics, again treating visual material that I had selected. A geometric scheme probing the relationship between cube, circle and triangle, already a textual feature, was accentuated in some of the designs, to great effect.

* * * * *

Basil Bunting noted the limitations of the modernist tendency to be extensively referential.[14] This would apply particularly to a long poem such

---

[14] 'A Conversation with Basil Bunting' in *Poetry Information* 19 (Autumn 1978), 40

as *The Cantos*. Later practice perhaps permits more ambient significance. Allen Fisher uses the term 'float perception' to describe a situation where 'immediacy from an attentive reader takes precedence over any deeper meaning obtained through in-reading'.[15] My own work is often densely allusive but it's intended to be read as available surface too. Specific cultural and historical references are subsumed within a different order of language – as indicated by Veronica Forrest-Thomson when she cites Wittgenstein's remark: 'Do not forget that a poem, even though it is composed in the language of information is not used in the language-game of giving information'.[16] An example of the trickiness of allusion is the phrase 'You were borderline' in *Roxy*, section 37:

First there was a garden with perfect slabs
of grass, trimmed privet cones
and a criss-cross of gravel walks.
The figures were statues on pedestals,
a stucco hand holding a cluster of grapes.
Then you were there leaning
against the balustrade, almost stone
but not, a breathing space between sentences.
You were borderline, breaking a familiar
armour, as glass turns right into left,
solids into liquid, touch into see.   (89)

Although H.D.'s description of Astrid in the film *Borderline* may be recalled, the words do not – by virtue of their surrounding matter – have this as a main connotation or level of interest. With shift of pronoun and tense, the phrase has gone over into something else, still carrying part of its specific literary or film context.

When I read in Buffalo in 1997 Robert Bertholf referred to 'the fragments' he had heard me perform. I discovered that he meant *Southam Street*,[17] a shorter sequence, but the term is an apt description of my structural method: holding different or dispersed entities in a tense relation, creating a grid which allows for contact and ignition through a variable scale of possibility. Each sectional unit within my book length

---

[15] Allen Fisher, *Imperfect Fit: Aesthetic Function, Facture, and Perception in Art and Writing since 1950* (University of Alabama Press, 2016), 49
[16] *Poetic Artifice* (Manchester University Press, 1978), x
[17] New River Project, 1991; included in *Music's Duel*, 109-118

poems has some coherence in itself but means more in the larger frame of the work.

The books vary in form, their character partly dictated by what might (misleadingly) be called 'the subject'. However, there are elements of continuity. Although progression often goes against the linear, each work has a significant narrative dimension. Historical contexts are implicitly or overtly presented in relation to more recent or contemporary events. While larger structural modes operate, I remain deeply engaged with linguistic fabric at a local level, seeking a register that goes beyond everyday patterns of speech while still retaining fluidity of expression. What might otherwise be information-heavy has a lyric strain and, I hope, a considerable measure of play.

Ken Edwards

Another Portrait: 73 sentences for Gavin Selerie

A portrait is valued by no one out of the family. He is a very persevering poet, whoever he is. I'll write a line presently. He is very glad to stay here, and confesses he is much better since he came. He is in love – desperately enamoured. The inexorable floor, the walls, the ceiling. Over this document, scanning it as lawyers do a new Act of Parliament, we took comfort. He verdant, violet to verdigris. Gavin shall have plenty of matter. You must direct where he shall walk. Yes, he says; I preferred the preliminary adjustment. He has resolved wisely and well. Almost stopping. Muttering to himself. He has never been anything but kind. As genius is never without its eccentricities, Selerie has his peculiarities, and among these, perhaps the most amusing, his rooted aversion to cursor, screen and printer. I felt myself blushing. This amiable young man, flowering. I am sure he thinks me a very impertinent fellow. We saw Beauty for the first time, throwing grain to the poultry. He tells tall tales. I may as well take a chair. It's a substitute for that which is not available or able to be indulged. There was a suspension. Here or there I omit or shorten passages and disguise names. I trace these lines with a trembling hand. The room a little darkened. My friend was the first (and last) poet I had ever seen. The name is out; but who is the man? He had been on the point of writing. So I am told. He done pixellated, done deeds in the hours of needs. Let his narrative stand. Oh don't, don't, *don't*, Mr Selerie, oh, no, no, no, no! Doctors never did him no good. Shocked at his prodigality, he hinted at a resonance, or maybe a residence. But no, he is not afraid. The house you leave is the house you make. He is not very rich. I can only tell you in a general way, it is so very long since I read it; but it was written in a kind of slang, and parts as hard to understand as a prize fight. Here are more verses. Which are the limbs, the hum of voices? I saw you dance an exhibition quadrille, you had a good measure. I may use my discretion in this. Is it a time to talk? I'll never call you a name. They know you here. There was no answer. This is the violation of letters! Were we pursued? Vivid evidence of the stern vicissitudes and insecurity of the times. Not looking half understanding and woefully bewildered, I dropped. The highest frequencies are erased in the cooking because it randomises the particles. It struck me that I recognised his features. He wrote a little book, the binding of which was mediaeval and costly. Language he would abolish.

He troubles himself little about it, I believe. He's harper or rhymer. I would go low to know such bounds. Yes, he is very well. I saw him as recently as March this year, and complimented him on his red hat. And the general ensemble. He discussed the relationship between Eric and Jerry. Someone lost his voice and another read his words. A lovely day: stressful, delightful, a slight disappointment, decent, unpretentious, dark, paradoxical, free, a great performance, in great spirits, with great vibrancy, cute, interminable, crowded and stuffy, not very good, excellent, very moving, rather trying and dense, rather good, rather nice, nice, brief and beautiful. We all had Covid. The flow's been hanging, and the resonance of the voice is alarming. We listened to Manfred Mann in the Great Hall once. Remember to write a piece for Gavin. I never thought you would go so low. That was Mr Bob Dylan, laureate of this parish. Sometimes melancholy is exactly what you need. We were waiting for the main act to start when the news came in.

(A continuation of 'A Portrait: 60 short sentences for Gavin Selerie', on the occasion of Gavin Selerie's 60th birthday, 2009, including found and treated material from Le Fanu's Ghost *and Sheridan Le Fanu's* Uncle Silas. *Thirteen sentences added. Written to further celebrate Gavin Selerie's life, St Leonards, October 2022.)*

Gavin Selerie, Elaine Edwards, Ken Edwards and the musician Charlie Morrow at 'Performed Poetics', an event at King's College London to commemorate the late Eric Mottram, March 2022.

John Goodby

from *So Rise*

A View

Historic sweet talk, soft
feats funding small marvels
in the firefly. Shrunk
extravert of gold current

among the corporeal
suits, my old emerald
cells soar to clap the future
brim with us.

The Seas

Being is proximity, a hard think
with plastic chip and chairs.

No windows call on me, the cell
is a dance of image, mobile sunlight

on the muscular wind. The whole
rainy phenomenon says work

with the other side to inhere
one truth or two, describe

equations on the rail of the arm,
metaphors that coincide as billions.

Dolphin

Out of the seven mahogany seas
our every colour in the shade

shines. Kiss, and synecdoche gives up
in that salty syllable the world works for

and has lodged in morality and force.
Anyone could show how love has me now.

Traditional

The last past insists, let's take
the now; we whistle a morning
to turn from fossil crossings over
lovers' affairs. Poet, how strong
have you sung an ocean?

Jeff Hilson

3 Self Portraits for Gavin Selerie

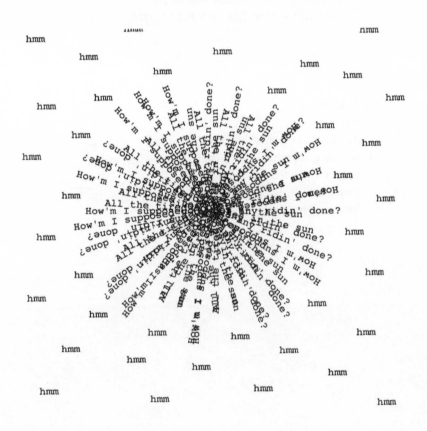

These are the words of a frontier lad

Who lost his love when he turned bad

These are the words of a frontier lad

Who lost his love when he turned bad

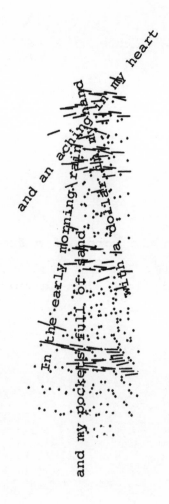

In the early morning, raining, with a dollar with my heart and an aching hand my pockets full of sand and my hand and my pockets full of sand

Lyndon Davies

Modal
(for Gavin)

After which he just goes on tinkering
at the keyboard just gently noodling, he doesn't know
what there is or could be something he couldn't find
if he knew, then the other wanders over tapping
on a cowbell to which the first harmonically
adapts and they go on doodling and then another
sidles over with a glass of brandy in his hand
starts pinging at it with a pencil and the note this makes
just happens to be – you're kidding – an exact octave
over the cowbell, then another sniffs
for whatever there is or something or half-feels for it
in its unofficial capacity and then another
comes sloping down from the control box as if already
hearing it in the mood to hear it, what could not be heard
yet but to coax from the gathering urge
in the metal the buzz in the weight of it and he joins them
gradually and they are joined and the thing
that never had even roughly
ever even slightly been there is now there
or thereabouts, in the fingers the mouths and there to be uncovered
in the muscles the joints the throats
and given its head and tracked but that doesn't matter
as long as the tape's running
the tape's running

Elaine Randell

With Grace

Just A Man
dazzled by light
his glossed plumage emits from a quiet home.
A heron startles against the scarlet flax,
that brace of skylarks lifts the lid as the nested poppy seeds
rupture
along the cliff edge where we hang
limp until poised again as memory chants us back
into the warm domestic relief.

Just A Man but Such a Man
dazzled by light
above a scree of gorse, yolk yellow
racing the slower heart. The buzzard clips
the ear of a soldier at dawn its mewing off spring.
A hedgerow
simply a hedgerow calls us back
for its tender jubilant chimes suggest
to only lay down among them, to be dazzled
that's all, just lay.

October 2022

David Miller

'Ink (for Gavin)', I

'Ink (for Gavin)', IV.
(Turn clockwise for the correct orientation.)

Amy Evans Bauer

Would be a falcon and go free

Gavin: variation on medieval name Gawain;
white hawk or falcon

Hat: Old English hætt, *of Germanic origin;*
related to Old Norse hǫttr *'hood'*

falcon flies
above woods

                    hood's finery
                    shines below —

claws that trod
hand track curb

                    from human heart
                    of pulse that soars

beyond the reach
of will, 'til blue

                    hills where
                    falcons nest

.

beyond words
bird glides

                    spies twitches
                    of bards' wrists

drawing blood
and scream

                              and to the west,
                              setting sun seems

human souls gone
not down in flames

                              but feathered, splayed
                              as wing across the edge

where sky and land
will seem to touch again

                              once dark is done,
                              lamps lit to furthered

reach of up up lifted
beak in song

104

Gregory Vincent St. Thomasino

Thinking
for Gavin Selerie

sight is to giving us to see
the voice, in absence

is giving us to see.
looking is to giving us to see

the coat, in absence
is giving us to see

the house, in absence
is giving us to see.

sight is to giving us to see
the face, in absence

is giving us to see
the sentence, in absence

a,
this is to giving us to see

Gillian Allnutt

Pencil Sketches for a Portrait of the Poet

In the Refectory, Kings Manor, York

'Not soup bowl: ecuelle'
he says,
my diffident medievalist.

very fine smooth translucent paper (OED)

'There are spheres, celestial,
seven of them, seen through –'
Note on onionskin.

Roughage

Gusts in grasses. Muster of
Grass and ghost and graces.
World without edge.

A note on the poems

Gavin and I met on the PGCE course 1972–3 at Sussex University and did our teaching practice together at Midhurst Grammar School where some wag dubbed us 'Walnut and Celery'. We both became teachers but really we were poets and carried on as such.

What I have really valued in Gavin through all the years is precisely the way he has kept faith with the poet in himself, working with such precision and patience somewhere on the edge of the world. This has been an invaluable source of support to me and I am truly grateful.

The haiku here are three out of forty I wrote one winter when working at the University of York, a place I remember was significant for Gavin. I hope they have caught something of my own sense of the essence of him.

Paul Holman

Azimuth Fragments

From the winter solstice of 2017 until the summer solstice of 2022, I worked on a book which documented a series of ritual actions performed at sites associated with serpent and dragon legends in Sussex. As Gavin and I were both aware, this involved my visiting locations, such as Saint Leonard's Forest and the Knucker Hole at Lyminster, which had featured in his own *Azimuth*. In the following text, I shadow his path through the Steyning section of that book, extracting a line from each successive page.

*

Laiden with spiky husks,
a body crushed and folded.

He used twigs of elder to drive his cart,
that rises as the smoke from Shoreham chimneys.

In wild, human voice,
a description of satyric cries,
the disc on the turntable not for hearing.

A shaft through six seams of flint,
a small bowl carved from a lump of chalk.

Lilies
        sprang up where this saint's blood fell,
as by woefull experience it was
                        proved.

The pool is cold in summer but never freezes.
He found his shoes covered in mud
                        and blades of grass.

All the books on the restricted list
would be out of character in
                        Steyning.

He had adders
                hanging round his neck
in
    the dark, while lights shine on mirrors and coloured
                                   frames.

Arms but no hands, and legs but no feet,
kept in a long thin box
                upon which I scratched.

I go to ground; my own country seems foreign,
and circumstances were difficult.

So clean and orderly, moving along well-worn paths,
all those suicides and sudden deaths.

Set
    them under the altar, sing over them nine hymns
every morning fasting.

Susana Medina

Oh, Gavin Selerie...

We're neighbours, I said.
And close, spiritually, you said.

I wanted to phone you, and I did, and say
you're so gentle & playful
& silly & serious
& delicate & skinny
& honest
& polyphonic.
With your fedora hat on, you will perform the ultimate magic trick.
You might even want to wear your flaming red shirt
and hold your prescribed glass of red wine.

Oh, trying not to think about it, you said.
Would you like me to visit?
In three weeks' time, the writingholic said.

It was good to talk for a long time this August.
Sharing secrets, as usual,
merci thank you.
And you told me about the autobiography you were writing
about your wild youth,
and soon after, I bumped into Frances, who looks forever young,
her face, an afterimage these days.

I could hear your voice answering the phone,
Always a little laughter, reverberating after each sentence.

We met at your madness and poetry class
At Mary Ward Centre, after which, many a pint,
Elizabethan poetry and Joyce,
mingled with a luscious texture of poetic traditions from all times,
enlightening Monday evenings
in cosy The Queens Larder (named after Queen Charlotte,
wife of the 'Mad King' George III, who was receiving treatment for
his apparent insanity at a doctor's house in the square)
while we good students bought rounds and rounds.
Then, Jubilee Line, back home, the spark of many a conversation.

Will you please send me a sign?
Pull out a couple of inches your *Le Fanu's Ghost* on my bookshelf?

Tilla Brading

Thank you, Gavin

Sitting reading under a standard lamp or beneath an Anglepoise, walking light ruck-sacked and light-footed on Quantock, Exmoor and Dorset paths, enjoying wine, giving readings, attending conferences, of the academy, railing against the academy, silhouetted against the sea.

When Gavin and Frances Presley first visited us Derrick Woolf, my then partner, was custodian of Coleridge Cottage (the poet's home from 1797 to 1800) and running Odyssey Poets Press. Gavin and Derrick shared interests in architecture, Hawksmoor and Geoffrey Grigson.

Gavin's poem, 'Of Mausolus', originally published in *Figs* 10 (c1986) refers to the mausoleum at Castle Howard designed by Hawksmoor:

> Spring on the brink
> of a steep balk, no shiver
> in the lake beside.
>
> I was at iron gates
> the hill I stepped up
> massing dark against sky:
> drum and dime, rising
> from another, wider,
> its columns crowded
> with Artemesia's yearning.
>
> I reached out
> a form and figure durable
> if anything is so
> in this world.

Over the years Gavin and Frances came to stay with us or nearby many times in Nether Stowey and later, Minehead, where Frances had lived as a teenager. She and I developed several writing and performance collaborations, and Gavin frequently came walking with us particularly in search of stones (for *Stone Settings* [FP & TB]), trees (*Halse for Hazel* [FP]), Ada Lovelace (ADADADA [FP, TB) and coastal landscapes which have informed our collaborations and individual work. We also met at readings, at many of which Gavin contributed – Birkbeck, Crossing the Line, Shearsman, Tears in the Fence (a Covid Zoom) & Poetry Picnics for example.

I'm pleased to be drawn to Gavin's 'Statement on Poetry' in the Archive of the Now (https://www.archiveofthenow.org/authors/?i=123) and have taken the liberty to use it as a starting point for the following appreciation:

Layering of voices Interlaced or Overlaid

(for 2 voices reading separately then concurrently)

layering of voices sitting reading

through history and landscape under a standard lamp

magic, mischief, invention beneath an Anglepoise

cut the abstract noun walking light

except where it tells ruck-sacked

a spell residing light-footed

in an uttered shape over Quantock

any 'spirit excursion' over Exmoor

subject to enquiry of Dorset paths

lyric conditions questioned enjoying wine

vision interrupted giving readings

measures found in salvage attending conferences

gaps, silences, traces of the academy

interlaced or overlaid railing against

the pleasure of turning silhouetted

twisting language against the sea

the agony of getting it right

self and a force of emotion

not simply anecdotal or confessional

A serious game, a gamesome gravity.

layering of voices sitting
reading through history
landscape under a standard
lamp magic
mischief, invention beneath
anglepoise cut
the abstract noun walking
light except where it tells
ruck-sacked a spell residing
light-footed in an uttered shape
over Quantock any 'spirit excursion'
over Exmoor subject
enquiry of Dorset
paths lyric conditions
questioned enjoying
wine vision interrupted
giving readings measures
found in salvage attending
conferences, gaps, silences,
traces of the academy
interlaced overlaid railing
against the pleasure turning
silhouetted twisting
language against the sea

the agony of getting it right
self and a force of emotion
not simply anecdotal or confessional
A serious game, a gamesome gravity.

Gavin was one of the contributors to the *Canting Academy* edited by David Annwn in 2007. This was my contribution to a shared enjoyment:

Venus de Milo

crust of bread

Barnet fair
mince pies
once a week
North and South   oily rag

~~Margate Sands~~   ~~Chalk Farms~~   ~~Margate Sands~~

jam tart
(tittle –tattle)

cousin Wellie

(CANT)

bacon and eggs   scotch pegs
plates of meat

This is Gavin's hat placed on the medieval boundary stone marking the Old Cleeve and Brompton parish boundary in West Somerset, near the source of the River Tone. It is known as Naked Boy. (Probably taken in early 2000s.)

Photographs by Tilla Brading

Ian MacFadyen

Reading Gavin Selerie's *Roxy* (1996)

X She shapeshifts from shopgirl to showgirl, from street to stage, catwalk to screen… She's a seamstress and an office worker, a dancer and an artiste by any other name… And then the interchangeability of roles as she is remade and remodelled and daydreams a Cinderella scenario – 'Sewing your self into the stuff, / you dream you'll wear it to the ball…'

X The writer poses with her new hardback product, her work 'erotic, not clinical', her mission 'to write something / which will take readers / out of their lives…' But she's stuck with the publishing schedule of her own life: 'Once the book is out the work begins… signing session and photo shoots.' Like her own blueprinted stories, this is a script she is helpless not to follow, an inventory of literary festivals, book shop promotions, talk show interviews – in other words, going down the market place to trade. 'I don't write to a formula,' she claims, but blithely keeps 'the brand names and so on.' Her success as a writer has provided her with an Axminster carpet and a marble fireplace, but book titles proliferate exponentially and there's a flood of returns from the corporate glut, 'books sold backwards to middle-middlemen'. The warehouse remainders are towed away, and it's a short trip from skip to tip. Truth is, the product was pulp from the beginning, every text a potential tax write-off, every writer an expendable asset.

X And then an alternate, terrifying literary take, a real auto-da-fé: a book's 'boards splayed out like wings', its pages melting and congealing in fire – creativity, talent, imagination and delight flaming from a petrol-soaked heaven-struck pole.

X 'Come on, after meat and drink / our first want is decoration…' but self-adornment and self-projection and re-creation may be only surface manoeuvres, as Selerie is aware: 'Before I was this I was a hippie, / before that a mod. / I was on the road in denims and shades / but it wasn't exactly the dustbowl look.' But the young women of *Roxy* often need their jobs and wages and must submit to the demands and codes of social and cultural fashion, reversing Selerie's line, 'Not about necessity but choice…'

X Fashion is omnipresent. Paul Buck comments on fashion cuttings in *A Public Intimacy (A Life Through Scrapbooks)* (2011): 'Today classy image shots have become part of news items.' Now fashion isn't just in the news –

it is the news, and everything that fits is instantly re-cut and re-transmitted. 'This is the diet of the times... a duffle coat at the cenotaph.'

X Doomed Flower Children plunder a dressing-up costume box – Victorian tat and Edwardian pastiche, fine threads and customized rags, the scrim dreams of some vaudeville shadow show. Soon enough these heritage clichés will be fashion curated and mediated, a hybrid conflux of styles glossily remade and remodelled – 'This over centuries, millennia is all / there for wearing.'

X More than a pathology of poshlost or the burlesque follies of some magazine zeitgeist, there is also recreation of self as the flash and glow of truly artistic inspiration and discovery: 'Je est un autre...' Despite 'the price of / everything that breathes', Gavin Selerie writes of 'a self not bounded / with clothes or skin', and 'You have to keep casting off the mask / to find who you are', to create or discover a self which may escape the parameters of cultural identification and market analysis. Even those seemingly consumed by the fashion system may somehow persist and get through: 'She is what she wears, is sold / and retains her soul.'

X The economic forces behind fashion are confronted – 'Only a vertically integrated multinational / is geared up to survive' in post-industrial Britain, 'a foreign fabric cut by laser / and sent back to be sewn and finished.' That 'inspired cutting' is the guarantor of credit circulating from Paris to London, Tokyo and Milan, and this 'trim show' is run by brokers or 'buzzards' on a promissory note.

X These unknown heroines have necessary recourse to the mirror, but self-reflection and self-examination create a continually changing mosaic of cut-up images of self, preparing women for the apotheosis of cinematic editing: 'Girls get used to chopped-up images: / eyes, nose and mouth in a powder compact, / the back of the head in a hand mirror, / feet and ankles in shop glass.' The mirror is 'a portable universe' and 'The enemy in the mirror is your self / or your friend.' But mirror transformation is endless: 'Out of mirrors, lights and scents, / the promise to change is bought / and endlessly deferred.'

X The poet sees books sliced and diced, cut to order to furnish a lifestyle ad for a luxury pad. 'But when shall we actually write books like catalogues?' (Walter Benjamin, *One-Way Street*). Selerie was reading Charles Olson, Ted Berrigan, Ed Dorn, Tom Raworth and the new British radical poetics, works totally off all industry radar. Try casually placing *Maximus* or *Gunslinger* on a side table in a glossy *nature morte* photo shoot for a superior brand of whisky or perfume.

X Media language is made plain and serviceable, 'an identikit real whose meaning self / can be lectured out / in stages...' The 'ready-worded' is 'mind furniture', 'a trust-me discourse' with a 'puffed one-liner / robustly upsending / a robust nothing', it's a lingua franca 'determined by committee' or a 'reigning sub-editor'. Like sham, tawdry garments, 'The whole matter is a woven text / put on and then put off... every line a would-be jewel.' But those word-jewels are dull paste and the text falls apart at the seams.

X For Selerie the true work of writing is beyond mass distribution, it 'may be lifted from unswept corners' and 'passed round, samizdat' while 'the non-work is sold, with bonuses / over one noisy counter.' *Roxy* is not scribbled and scripted 'in instant meaning' though the poet knows that 'A text that departs from the lavender sachet / is gulled, or worse, ignored.' The injunction is to 'Take off this value-language / for under that you may see beauty.' Rather than concealing editing in some seamless narrative, Selerie foregrounds his talismanic word juxtapositions, multi-layered time shifts, dissolving views and highly visual jump-cuts. *Roxy* is textually lush, seductive, biting, and etymologically tricky, and Selerie relishes his themes of camouflage, disguise and simulation, driven by alarm and disgust with corporate blank speak and machinic psuedo-transparent prose.

X The voices of the models, actors, and working women in *Roxy* transmute and mutate just as their garments are adopted and discarded – it's a work of 'voice shifting into voice', as Selerie writes of Rushdie's *Satanic Verses*. The characters are nameless – they are the manifest personas and sisters and daughters of the legendary Roxy, moving through the decade of 1985–1995 but radiating back through time, their anonymity neither stereotypical nor archetypal as each strives for her own individual, aspiring existence in the tawdry dazzle of the earthly fashion firmament – in their alienated and exploited situations 'the grit and the glitz ran together'. They cannot resist the Model Directory, the dress rehearsal, the chance of a lifetime, they cannot break free from those roles which may seem chosen but turn out to be existential impositions. No kind of stylistic reinvention will permit them release from their allotted span and their seemingly fixed place in the social order of things. They shine, they suffer, they endure, they disappear.

X It was from the cultural mélange of 1960s London – the mixing and matching of pop stars, politicians, gangsters and fashion models in a dangerous new milieu of money, sex and drugs – that the modern Fashion Age was created and from which Donald Cammell's film *Performance* (1968/72) emerged. The Saddle Room, Hamilton Place, Mayfair was the first discothèque in London and by 1962 it was the hangout of the 'Chelsea Set': 'people connected with the rag trade, and, noticeably, a great many fashion models,' noted George Melly. Many clubs followed, including the Scotch of St James's, Duke Street and the UFO on Tottenham Court Road, some exclusive, some not, but all were places to be seen on the scene, to preen and promote and perform and be photographed. The Ad-Lib, Leicester Square was 'dedicated to the triumph of style', the clothes reflecting 'Carnaby Street at its most extreme'. Although not specifically invoked in Gavin Selerie's *Roxy*, it is this period and *Performance* in particular which marked the most profound and radical change in the psychology of fashion and opened up the area of gender and identity politics. *Roxy* seems in crucial ways a work which is thematically and philosophically bound up with Cammell's concerns about images of self and style and the projection of the psyche.

X James Fox wouldn't talk to me about *Performance*. It was the 1970s, and the film still held disturbing memories for him – no, it just wasn't possible. Instead we talked about the charming 1950 film *The Magnet*, his first starring role at the age of eleven, under the name William Fox. But three decades later Anita Pallenberg was happy to discuss the film. A successful model and actress, tabloid infamy and damnation were among the prices she would have to pay for fame and freedom and Cammell's film was often invoked as the decadent violent paradigm of her own 'downfall'. It was the greatest British film of all time, Anita said, and the first and most important film of self-recreation, exploring appearance and illusion, and sexual and gender identity in ways that transcended 'just dressing up and all that.' She was proud of her contribution and spoke of the film with passion – 'It won't be forgotten.' Anita, who was studying photography at St Martin's when I met her, showed me photos she'd recently taken in JouJouka in Morocco, and somehow managed to set her shoulder bag on fire, emptying out its contents onto the courtyard – 'I've been meaning to sort that thing out for years.'

X Anita played the part of Pheber in *Performance*, and she was from the start the incarnation of the spirit which Donald Cammell drew on for his counter-cultural vision, but the result was the creation, both on and off screen, of a third undifferentiated persona, a Pheber/Pallenberg twin soul born from the conjunction of actress and role. 'People kind of always see me like that, I'm sure,' she said, 'it's sort of deadly… But I don't think about it.' Pallenberg/Pheber is imperious and capricious, provocative, hedonistic, merciless, courageous and innocently wondering, freed from all constraint and imposition… Anita said that for her the 1960s was the crucial time – the freedom to play and experiment and reinvent one's way of living before puritanical reaction and moral condemnation set in. Now the 1960s was again being recuperated and regurgitated by the media in ways she found laughable, pathetic and sad, a counterfeit designer dumb show. She did not recognize herself in 'all the rubbish written about me' nor in the reframing of her own recycled image as fashion icon – 'the beauty of the '60s' was true, but it left her indifferent. Her life was more than that fur jacket or plastic raincoat, 'but that's the way it is now and will always be.' Her image was fixed forever in the public mind and press and even Marianne Faithfull's wry, affectionately intended tribute in her 1994 memoir would be quoted to confirm the worst: 'Courtfield Road, Brian Jones and Anita Pallenberg's flat... A veritable witches' coven of decadent illuminati, rock princelings and hip aristos... At the centre like a phoenix on her nest of flames... the wicked Anita.'

X Nothing is untouched by the fashion system – both clothes and bedrooms are 'fitted' while colour coordination may extend to a jacket and skirt or the twin reception rooms in a starter home sold as a set for the acting out of lifestyle and status. It's the final fruition of Georg Simmel's theory of the imitative conformity of metropolitan actors, with money as determinant of human values and beliefs. There is no escape from the fashion chain – those who refute fashion and claim to be entirely themselves are actually engaged in an inverse form of imitation and their own supposed uniqueness becomes simply another style. 'In the end they're all the same – / just different uniforms. / Style is what you can't deny / about yourself.' Still, fashion is always finally retrograde, a losing game, running out of time, consigning us haplessly to history: 'Fabric gives birth to what you want. / Nitrates crumble to dust. / The more of the moment you are / the more of the past you become.'

X In *How Modernity Forgets* (2009), Paul Connerton articulates the split between hypermnesia (too much remembering) and the structures of forgetting that are built into contemporary experience. The transmission of cultural memory involves media and information processes which generate 'a particular kind of cultural amnesia'. Radio, press, television and social media continually produce and reprise edits from a chaos of archival materials and recycled histories, but these cultural manifestations of remembrance are undone by 'the post-mnemonic structures of the political economy', which repeatedly erase material experiences and cultural environments, destroying the lived experience of the streets. Significantly, Selerie writes: 'From cotton fields to the catwalk / you look for the master trope / in a lexicon of fropperies... Leaves eaten by a worm / are the memory of a world / without memory.'

X We see the dissolving views of a blue planet... Tele-machines flicker and electric doors whirr as a young woman moves through a spaceship wearing strange patchwork clothes like a Sonia Delaunay modernist take on Russian folk art – even in space the heroine must be styled... She smiles at the camera, watches a videotape of herself on a monitor, she is dead but continually brought back to life, a neutrino woman atomically reconstituted by a sea of liquid gas, a revenant who can still caress skin, an amnesiac who must be human because she is filled with pity and tenderness and she loves and desires to live, ceaselessly. ... This woman dies in order to be reborn, she levitates in her lover's arms, floating free of the image-repertoire, escaping gravity and the imposition of identity...

X Consumed by images, the speed of possible transformations is now vertiginous, beyond comprehension or realisation. The retina of the human eye can register ten new images every second. Digital systems stream tens of thousands of images far surpassing the proliferation of images created by colour printing. A single digital image grid based upon a permutation of eight (8 X 7 X 6 X 5 X 4 X 3 X 2 X 1) provides an order of 38,320 possible new styles and looks. Interconnecting permutations of shots produce enough modes to provide a new visual experience every tenth of a second for a lifetime.

X Reading *Roxy* reminds me of another actress whose unique, disturbing and ravishing artistry was diluted and recuperated by media. In a 1965 film review by Leonard Mosley the actress Monica Vitti was characterised as an Ice Maiden – although she was 'outer ice' she still burned, thankfully, with an 'inner fire'. Fascinating and enigmatic, and so problematic, the critic nevertheless concedes that she is a special 'female adornment' to the screen.

X Antonioni's *L'Eclise* premiered at the Cameo-Poly, Regent Street, in December 1963. The heroine, Monica Vitti in the role of Vittoria, has already vanished from this story of alienation and materialism before the mesmerising closing sequence... She is lost to us forever, the rest of her story never to be known... Sound of the wind, aerial view of empty suburban streets... Buildings under construction, light and shadow on blank postwar façades, running water in the streets, the sound of children's voices, passengers disembarking from a lone bus. ... The haunted looks of pedestrians, a man walking along reading *L'Espresso* as the lights come on at dusk and the passengers make their way home, darkness falling... The camera holds on a close up of a single blazing, ominous electric street light... **'FIN'**

London, October 2022

Gilbert Adair

Caxton's H: A Letter For Gavin

It is in their nature to multiply
(the letters shift)
I have journals and other papers

Gavin Selerie, *Le Fanu's Ghost*

Noteworthy about the Prologue to *Le Fanu's Ghost* (2006) is that besides an account of the intermarrying Le Fanu/Sheridan familial/literary nexus tracked to a level of detail, it presents a demystification of the Irish Gothic machinery with which eponymous author Sheridan Le Fanu is chiefly associated – driven in his case, we're told, by anxieties regarding both a range of suspect allurements and also security of inheritance (to do, as Robert Hampson notes, with the increasing precarity of the tortuously positioned Protestant Ascendancy to which both families belonged).[1] And there is a literary pedigree going back to Spenser and the Jacobean dramatists. The brisk accounting may leave us to wonder, *What then is the 'ghost' of the book's title?* And how is it given form for early 21st-century readers? I want to write enough here to suggest that there is a formal absent-presence built into the text of which Gavin was entirely conscious, and which makes this book, dealing mainly with 18th- and 19th-century Irish writers – although also, pervasively, Joyce – a thoroughly contemporary work.

None of this should imply that *Le Fanu's Ghost* has no interest in exploring (as opposed to explicating) passions that attach to the Gothic; after all, for a lost beloved, 'the light in the grave || begs to be written' (104). And at least for a while, it keeps begging: 'now the show / is over // it starts again' (236); there is clear recognition of the pleasure of telling, as Thomas Moore records, 'ghost stories to the ladies all the way home' (230), and that 'Your fright scene / is the comic gag / re-versed' (243). But more often, as Alice Rayner reminds us, 'Ghosts hover where secrets are held in time: the

---

[1] See Robert Hampson, 'Gavin Selerie's *Roxy* and *Le Fanu's Ghost*.' This article also provides a precisely detailed glimpse of the complex handlings of 'associative matrices' that structure both these long poems.

secrets of what has been unspoken, unacknowledged' (x) – see, for example, the sharply surprising turn taken by Gavin's 'Feelers' ('fingers white by moonlight calling / you are || this is / the moment / always known,' 74) – or secrets of debts unpaid, unfinished business. These, some Kildare locals believe, animate the thwarted love for Jonathan Swift of the dead Hester Vanhomrigh ('Vanessa'), who can be seen at midnight in a certain locale 'with a dog and fire coming from its mouth' (166), and who reappears in the 'Words on the Window Pane,' where she shares with the other great thwarted love of Swift's life, Esther Johnson ('Stella'), 'a heart of melted lead and flaming pitch' (168). The poem takes off, of course, from Yeats's 1930 play *The Words Upon the Window-Pane*, which uses its setting of a séance disrupted by an anguished spirit (that of the Dean himself) to defend Swift's refusal to marry either Vanessa or Stella on the grounds that 'I have something in my blood that no child must inherit' – he speaks of 'constant attacks of dizziness' but implicit also is his 'saeva indignatio,' lacerating in face of a democratizing world where the virtues of a Brutus or a Cato are 'beaten down.'[2] Such is Swift's own account from beyond the grave – or that of the medium Mrs Henderson speaking in Swift's voice; demurring in her own that such a chaotic séance merits no payment but accepting the cash her attendees press upon her. In the matter of ghosts, that is, Yeats borrowed the solution of those 19th-century writers who offered readers of their supernatural fiction a rational out. But that misses the phantasmal reality that Gavin, I am arguing, seeks to bring into apprehension.

Let me backtrack for a moment to the book's first poem, 'Tomogram' (the image of a body's internal structure as displayed via wave interference). It opens with a 'text' (a text message?) whose provenance, indeed very existence, is in question,

> but since after all the message
> yields up
>
> Caxton's H
> a panel of ink starvation
> as seen in Gothic – 'ghastly for to see'
>
> the word is as much as breath
> at three removes

---

[2] W.B. Yeats, 'The Words upon the Window-Pane', 49; cf also 39–40, 48. For 'beaten down,' see Yeats's 1919 poem, 'The Fisherman.'

> beyond the jurisdiction of veracity
> paling in a spectral line (63)

Caxton was supposed to have inserted the silent 'h' in the word 'ghost'; the reference is taken up in 'Words on the Window Pane': 'that doubled STAR / drops an H.' (168) Interpretation is tenuous: 'Stella,' as Stanley Kowalski would remind his wife when he wanted something, means 'star'; both Esther (Stella) and Hester (Vanessa) – two variants of 'Esther' – lose an 'h' in Swift's recasting of their names ... the letter disappears, in any case, as abruptly as it first appeared. And 'Tomogram' loses no time in stressing that the 'spectral line' is 'nobody's flicker, that screen double / who crosses your brain // misread and so enshrined / the train outside the table // darts fire...' (63) We're dealing with a ghost at once of a person who isn't there and at the same time of no one at all: the ghost trains, perhaps, of the slowly commercializing Ireland that ghosted Molly Malone. The doubling is crucial: recall that 'character' can mean both letter and figure in a (dramatic) fiction – an ambiguity that *Le Fanu's Ghost* will exploit to the hilt.

Artaud is no doubt the pertinent theorist of theatres and doubles here, with his central insight that the contemporary 'culture idolatry' paradoxically functions 'as if there were culture on the one hand and life on the other' (3), as opposed to 'ancient Totems' which did not so much 'represent' the forces behind them as bear within them 'a double, a shadowed self' (5). We can get a late-19th-century glimpse of this in Edward Gordon Craig's biography of the actor Henry Irving, a book Gavin draws on for 'Lyceum Double (5.72).' This poem presents initially as a block of prose cut across by a blank diagonal from the upper left corner to lower right, which on closer inspection separates two prose segments, so that one may read the opening lines vertically, this side of the blank diagonal:

BELLS
what is
jangling
it is I – it is
the box open

or horizontally across from the diagonal, or from margin to margin:

<pre>
BELLS   HEARD is a sixteen-track remote bedded in the truck
what is   a blanket-lined tin for letters forming themselves
jangling   out of nowhere like ghost returns on a gone note
it is I – it is   the Master shows from Punchinello or snakes
the box open   your lucky STAR to match the festive eve... (299)
</pre>

The prose segments are divided visually; the horizontal syntax sometimes agrees but not always; the text emerges as a divided entity whose parts intermittently bleed into each other – a formal allegory of the actor playing his role. But note that Irving is already 'larger than life,' his entrance marked by applause 'so instantaneous,' Craig says, 'that it became part of the play' (54) – in this case *The Bells* by Leopold Lewis, which opened at London's Lyceum Theatre on 25 November, 1871. Irving plays Mathias, who 15 years earlier, his child starving, has murdered a wealthy Polish Jew who stops at his hut for shelter one snowstorm night. Mathias will go on to prosper, becoming the village Burgomaster, but remains haunted by the ever-unpredictable sound of the sledge-bells of his victim.

'The thing Irving set out to do,' writes Craig, 'was to show us the sorrow which slowly and remorselessly beat him down.... to wring our hearts' (57–58). On Mathias's entrance – after 'getting rid of his coat and brushing off the snow as he stands on the mat by the door ... [and] put[ting] on and buckl[ing] his shoes,' so slowly that 'in every gesture, every half move, in the play of his shoulders, legs, head, and arms, mesmeric ... we were drawn to watch every inch of his work' (58) – he realizes that those present have been talking about the 15-year-old murder, on a night as snow-blown as this one; and then, in Gavin's assemblage,

> ... will sweat clear suspicion
> and follow feedback frenzy postures
> BEAT by a bridge spritely vanished
> in deadspeak a bit underground (299)

Craig comments in a footnote, 'You will say, perhaps, that Irving explains so much to us that the other characters in the play were daft not to notice too" – but that is precisely the point:

Irving followed the most ancient and unshakable tradition, which says that the dramatist is to take his [sic] audience into his confidence ... [with] little or no thought paid to whether the other characters on the stage overhear or see. (61)

The enemy to Irving's 'heroic style' of acting is 'realism,' for the realist actor seeks to disappear behind or within the character, occulting the character as the actor's double.[3] This is why, Rayner argues, we routinely miss the uncanny dimension of that doubled singularity which is performance on stage or screen (x), and why Artaud links realist theatre 'with our fossilised idea of a shadowless culture' (5), absent the exalting largeness of interpenetrations which theatre that matters should instil: Henry Irving is (and is not) Mathias is/is not the open box is/is not the bells are/are not the 'letters forming themselves / out of nowhere.'

We're in sight again of that 'double meaning' of 'character' and the concomitant theatrical ability to produce 'people' by linguistic performance. Shakespeare's comedies repeatedly feature assumed (in both senses, if by different people) identities; in *Othello*, Iago speaks (and 'evidences') an alternative Desdemona into being. It's less the actor's double than the character's, split off and brought within the stage action; Sheridan's plays are full of this, to the point where the ironically named Captain Absolute in *The Rivals* generates in himself one of his own competitors for the hand of Lydia Languish (Language?). Gavin makes the irony clear in 'Rivals Interleaved', a cut-up of *The Rivals* and *The School for Scandal*: 'Ah, the gazettes of the Bath, the very men I want.... Oh, no foundation. People *will* talk' (184). But this poem also incorporates faux pas from Mrs Malaprop, including her sublime 'allegory on the banks of the Nile' (184), and perhaps more important to *Le Fanu's Ghost* than Richard Brinsley's plays is *The Art of Punning* (1719) by his father, Dr Thomas Sheridan – noted in Gavin's 'Personalia' as a 'friend and correspondent of Swift, his partner in language games; their journal *The Intelligencer* notable for its critique of English policy in Ireland'; while his influence is indicated on another of Gavin's master texts, *Finnegans Wake*, with its reference to 'Sharadan's Art of Panning' (348).

Thomas first then, and what I take to be the relevant rules of punning cited by Gavin:

---

[3] I don't want to play down the complexity of 'suspension of disbelief,' in Coleridge's invaluable phrase: anyone immersed in watching a narrative per-formance can register the fine delivery of a line, say, or an apt gesture, just as one can admire a nice turn of phrase in however 'realistic' a novel; we are talking here of tendencies, not absolute states of mind. See Ron Silliman's useful revision of his 1974 essay 'Disappearance of the Word Appearance of the World' in '"Postmodernism": Sign for a Struggle, Struggle for the Sign,' esp. 37.

Rule 14. *The Rule of Transition*: Which will serve to introduce any thing that has the most remote relation to the subject you are upon. ...

Rule 29. *The Hypothetick Rule*, is when you suppose things hardly consistent to be united for the sake of a pun. (142–43)

Rayner contrasts the 'ghostly double' for its involving 'secrets and a return' with a metaphor, although the latter 'also joins two unlike entities in a single image' (x); but a pun, which has only to sound or look like the target word or phrase, can play over a far wider range of content than either; we might say, as Gavin does of a text with another 'brought in' which 'threatens / to explode' it, 'the whole / is only / the holding / coordinates' (168).[4] Thus Joyce can turn Dante's bolge to 'ellboge' and shunt 'elbow' *Inferno*-wards:

> [T]he flaxen Gygas tapped his chronometrum drumdrum and, now standing full erect, above the ambijacent floodplain, scene of its happening, with one Berlin gauntlet chopstuck in the hough of his ellboge (by ancientest signlore his gesture meaning: ∃!) ... (36.13–17)

'Gygas' is Greek for 'giant', but he's also 'flaxen', a pointer echoed in 'Berlin'; might the 'ancientest signlore his gesture meaning: ∃!' evoke the Sanskrit svastika appropriated by National Socialism with its gestural trappings and the sign's own potential for ominous reversal? '[D]rumdrum' (there's an Irish town Dundrum) conjures a collective or ritual context, but perhaps, as Jacques Mailhos argues, for the ur-language of gesture theorized by Marcel Jousse, whose lectures Joyce attended in the 1930s, as well as the sigla that constituted Joyce's late-developed memory system (61–62); while the 'floodplain, scene of its happening,' evokes a range of world myths focused not on origin but (post-flood) a rebeginning. Such impacted polysemy in a thick sonic scrumptiousness is why Jed Rasula faults 'personifying HCE as "Earwicker"' for 'anthropomorphizing' the work's 'carnival of letters' (521, 522). It's not uninteresting that 'characters' are discernible in the *Wake*, and a 'plot' arguably concerning an inter- and then intra-generational struggle

---

[4] The original needs to be seen here, with its variety of fonts and font-sizes. I should also note that this poem, 'Faded Novel: Fine Again' (110–12), consists of a parody of Joyce's style in *Finnegans Wake*, a bold move; as the poet remarks later, 'To fear an acre is never to go' (128).

for the right to define, in Roy Benjamin's reading, what constitutes 'noise' and what 'harmony'; but Benjamin agrees that this struggle can't be ended; meaning is to be wrested, if at all and provisionally, from the cacophony of the world's 20th century ('Friday afternoon in the universe,' Jack Kerouac begins his homage to *Finnegans Wake*, *Old Angel Midnight*).

This, then, from Gavin (via William Ireland, a 'forger of Shakespearean manuscripts … after exposure and confession, made career as Gothic novelist') (337):

> I brought forth this not-undigested
> not-unconnected medley
> and men of superior genius
> believed the Bard alone was author (210)

It's possible to think of *Le Fanu's Ghost* as a breaking-down and separating-out of components of *Finnegans Wake*, but only as a step to appreciating the text's substantially different vision. There's a range of types of poems here: tight paratactic numbers like 'Tomogram' or, at the book's other end, 'André Breton Dreams the Walk of Charles Maturin' (309); mixes of other texts ('Rivals Interleaved'); filchings of styles – 'Belfast Blues' (219–20), 'Amarantha Takes' (237–38: Gothic erotica), or 'Skullscape' (276), which begins in a Beckettian voice and ends like a Bloom soliloquy but rougher; poems in two columns, often lists ('Alphacrux,' 256), or single-column lists such as 'Drury Nights' (214–16), naming plays put on at the Theatre Royal, 1794–1809; concrete poems and poems on Irish history, on which more imminently; and extended, virtually unedited passages from journals, letters, memoirs, and novels of the extended Le Fanu and Sheridan clans – also, of course, 'Irish-historical' materials. But here's where we touch the *Wake* again, for these prose pieces and, say, 'Drury Nights' arguably constitute 'noise,' insofar as they give insight into many of the leisure activities of cultured middle-class Protestants in 19th-century Ireland (with, yes, the financial ground eroding beneath them), and often indeed conclude with quietly pleasing payoffs, but as often have nothing to do with ghosts; and whose length may incite the question, 'How much of this is meant to be the point?!' As with the prose blocks Williams drops into the flow of *Paterson* like rocks in the falls, the answer of course is, 'All of it.'

In one sense, ghosts – the ghosts of unpaid, often unpayable debts – are the Irish story. 'Glass Master' provides a sketch of colonial and pre-colonial violence in Ireland, going back not only to Spenser ('an undertaker planted

West,' 78) but to the 12th-century (originally oral) *Táin Bó Cúailnge* or *Cattle-Raid of Cooley* –

> this is the bull
> taken as blunder
> that tells hub to rim
> what reckoning
> beckons (82)

– with its pitiless burden (the bulls whose bringing-together serves as pretext for the massive raid end up killing each other) that war has no winners. But the Sheridan/Le Fanu family/literary nexus is a strangely arbitrary way to approach this, not to mention that one result is poems often enticing (say, 'Duelling Tales,' 188) but whose 'backstory' lies in some obscure text which few if any of the book's readers are likely to consult – as Gavin must know, indeed intend; after all, most of the information we routinely take in and maul into coherence is extracted from massively unknown contexts; in the laconic summation of 'Polesden Lacey' (the other 'Irish history' set-piece), 'there are many dark actors playing games' (196).

But as Allen Fisher insists, while a serious poet's materials may be arbitrary (Gavin: 'I first saw the name Le Fanu on brass plaques in the chapel and on rugger boards in the East Portico at Haileybury [public school]...' 58), his or her 'aesthetic practice, whose patterns of connectedness are an insistent ground' (100), is not. The 'h' in 'ghost' is and is not there – quite like a ghost: we don't hear it when we hear the word; we see it, if at all, as an element of the word's shape, that is, we don't see it either. Ghosts are real to the extent that our lives are, factually, animated by truck with all sorts of dead, and Rayner is right that a good performer can 'unforget' – bring into apprehension – 'the presence of something absent, whether that be called a text or a character, history or the past' (xvi). And the closer-knit the group presented, the more liable to be squeezed out between and around it some awareness of the many, many not there. But a ghost can't close the gap of a 'national history' that throws up text after text in diversionary insistence, and Jameson is also right that art in this 'postmodern' age must address its own 'awareness of incommensurable distances within its object of thought' (168). As Gavin helpfully cites from Foucault's 1963 essay 'Language to Infinity,' 'the language of terror is dedicated to an endless expense' (54), not least when there seems no cause for it in a given locale. The art object coheres, again, by means of its 'holding coordinates,' and *Le Fanu's Ghost* finds one of its own synecdoches in the brilliant concrete poem 'Ligature' (279):

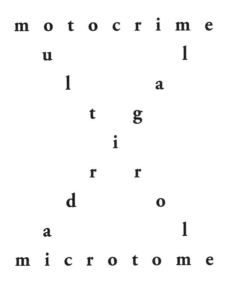

WORKS CITED

Artaud, Antonin. *The Theatre and Its Double* (1938), tr. Victor Corti, in *Collected Works* Volume Four, 1–110. London: Calder & Boyars, 1974.

Benjamin, Roy. 'Noirse-Made-Earsy: Noise in *Finnegans Wake*.' *Comparative Literature Studies*, Vol. 50, No. 4 (2013), 670–87. https://www.jstor.org/stable/pdf/10.5325/complitstudies.50.4.0670.pdf?refreqid=fastly-default%3Ac7c75cf0f3175cff01ab0e627418d6b5&ab_segments=0%2Fbasic_search_gsv2%2Fcontrol&origin=search-results&acceptTC=1.

Craig, Edward Gordon. *Henry Irving*, 1930. https://archive.org/details/in.ernet.dli.2015.209322/page/n85/mode/2up.

Fisher, Allen. 'Postmodernism as Practice.' *Poetics Journal* No. 7 (Sept. 1987), 100–04.

Foucault, Michel. 'Language to Infinity.' In *Language, Counter-Memory, Practice: Selected Essays and Interviews*. Ithaca, NY: Cornell University Press, 1977, 53–67.

Hampson, Robert. 'Gavin Selerie's *Roxy* and *Le Fanu's Ghost*,' http://jacketmagazine.com/36/r-selerie-rb-hampson.shtml. 2008.

Jackson, Rosemary. *Fantasy: The Literature of Subversion*. London: Routledge, 1981.

Jameson, Fredric. *Postmodernism, or, The Cultural Logic of Late Capitalism*. Durham, NC: Duke University Press, 1991.

Kerouac, Jack. *Old Angel Midnight*. London: Midnight Press, 1988.

Mailhos, Jacques. "'Begin to Forget It": The Preprovided Memory of *Finnegans Wake*.' *European Joyce Studies*, Vol. 4 (1994), 41–67. https://www-jstor-org.kauaiproxy.lib.hawaii.edu/stable/pdf/44870951.pdf?refreqid=excelsior%3Aef922c4478ccc7971af26f06ef4a605e&ab_segments=&origin=&acceptTC=1.

Rasula, Jed. '*Finnegans Wake* and the Character of the Letter.' *James Joyce Quarterly*, Vol. 34, No. 4 (Summer, 1997), 517–30. https://www.jstor.org/stable/pdf/25473842.pdf?refreqid=fastly-default%3Aa747bb44727b6fe058ccffde282814c8&ab_segments=0%2Fbasic_search_gsv2%2Fcontrol&origin=search-results.

Rayner, Alice. *Ghosts: Death's Double and the Phenomena of Theatre*. Minneapolis, MN: University of Minnesota Press, 2006.

Selerie, Gavin. *Le Fanu's Ghost*. Hereford: Five Seasons Press, 2006.

Silliman, Ron. '"Postmodernism": Sign for a Struggle, Struggle for the Sign.' *Poetics Journal* No. 7 (Sept. 1987), 18–39.

Williams, William Carlos. *Paterson*. London: MacGibbon & Kee, 1963.

Yeats, W.B. *The Words upon the Window-Pane: A play in one act with notes [by Yeats] upon the play and its subject*. https://archive.org/details/wordsuponwindowp0000yeat/page/48/mode/2up.

Anthony Mellors

Review of *Hariot Double*

Hariot Double. Gavin Selerie, Graphics by Alan Halsey.
Hereford: Five Seasons Press, 2016. Large format paperback.

The basics: Gavin Selerie's *Hariot Double* is a large-scale lyric sequence of poems focused on the life and work of the Elizabethan polymath Thomas Hariot and the Elizabethan jazz musician Joe Harriott. Apart from both living in the England of one Elizabeth or another, they appear to have little in common except similar surnames, and the initial question in titling / tilting the work must have been which version of the name to choose. Selerie's modus operandi is to fuse the tradition of English lyric with the longer tradition of pattern poetry, making him something of a postmodern George Herbert; so why does he plump for *Hariot Double* rather than Harriott / Hariot or Har(r)iot(t) or Ha(r)rio(t)t?[1] Serious though the underlying themes of the book are, with the doubling itself prompting questions of cultural and racial difference, colonialism and its legacy, and official versus 'barbaric' speech, the title's peculiarity is the first intimation of the ludic and humorous bent of the book. The formal principle of the work, almost Elizabethan in conception, is to yoke together two heterogeneous figures to see what strikes up. Harriott's medium is sound ('If abstract / who composed it'), Hariot's is vision ('Some See, Some Doe Not'); Harriott is a musical innovator, Hariot an inventor and mathematician: the differences are complementary, inviting readers to find possible connexions beyond the obvious and arbitrary similarity in names. One connexion might be a degree of marginalization shared by the two figures: Harriott's achievement on albums such as *Indo-Jazz Fusion* (1966) and *Hum Dono* (1969) was ahead of its time while being a perfect example of sixties far-outness, yet because of this innovativeness he seems to have become sidelined. Meanwhile, Hariot's privileged background did not prevent his intellectual experiments from being treated as dangerous and atheistic. If Harriott was working from the margins toward the centre of English-speaking culture ('Can I fluent Caliban / get accust, a-costumed'), Hariot moves from elite

---

[1] the typographer has addressed this issue in reverse on the verso facing the title page.

English origins to an eccentric vision of the New World ('there you lye beatynge upon ye shoale / with extreme hasarde of beying casteawaye'). The double narrative is in three sections, which quickly alert readers to a non-linear pattern. Harriott is first, Hariot last, concluding by falling into the hour of his birth. The two main sections are conjoined by an 'Intermean' (an early modern term for a transitional scene in a play), in which elements of the double theme mingle with more overtly autobiographical material. While this central section allows the two major discourses to intertwine (or basically do anything involving the prefix 'inter') and foregrounds the poet's researches, it's typically unclear as to who is speaking at any given moment or what is now and then or which then:

> There's no place for fancy stuff,
> throw the lumber over. Just need
> a lamp and sculls to get through
> or be born on the blarmed bit
> to understand.
>   ('Boat Spree')

Presumably this is the poet recounting a jaunt up the Thames from Kingston to Oxford as part of a field trip to Syon House, a 'Zion' historically relevant to Thomas Hariot in a number of ways and linking his 'Hampton, Kingston, Richemond / by farther curls, tyde-ruled' to Harriott's 'Richmond Revel' ('Two sweeps of river by the Old Deer Park') and back to his journey from Jamaica to Southampton. Indeed, the book's blue cover might be said to represent its preoccupation with river and sea voyages. The passage from 'Boat Spree' suggests description as metaphor for research. Yet the antiquated slang of 'blarmed' comes from the world of *Three Men in a Boat*, which also happens to be the 'record' of a trip from Kingston to Oxford. So the poet's voice – if the poet's voice it be – is always already confused with other texts, with which an experience – if that's what it is – is associated. Throughout, Selerie's use of voice, whether his own or personae or coming from documentary material (e.g., Harriott's girlfriend, and Pocahontas), is highly idiosyncratic and provisional, his style palimpsestic, cubist, overdetermined.

The proliferation of watery images and themes is too diverse to do justice to here, and I cannot attempt a synthetic analysis or detailed appraisal of the work in a review. This is something *Hariot Double* invites with its whole being, yet while such an horizon of structural unity is desirable, and is almost inevitably a feature of the long poem or sequence of poems, it is also something of a red herring, in that the fractured metonymies of the modernist epic are, as Charles Olson suggests, more about finding out for oneself and making new connexions than they are about reconstructing an intentional program from what is basically an assemblage. This problem of the poetic matrix occurs in a more secretive way with single lyric poems, with the matrix resurfacing in postmodern readings as a kind of disavowed New Criticism. That is to say, the poem continues to be interpreted even as the form of its saying (to fall back into vaguely phenomenological terminology) defies interpretation.

The first thing that should be noted is that this book, like Selerie's previous Five Seasons publication *Le Fanu's Ghost* (2006) and West House Books' *Roxy* (1996), is a distinctive, material object rather than a text made to fit into a 'house' style. While poetry is generally regarded as being in the mechanically reproducible sphere, its appearance on the page is always more than the printed representation of words, as readers of Bloodaxe publications will experience in a negative way. Complemented by Alan Halsey's brilliant graphics and perfectly supported by Glenn Storhaug's meticulous attention to production, *Hariot Double* feels concrete. It is a reproducible artist's book; concrete as graphic and ludic, but also in the sense of foundness, as in *musique concrète*. Visual elements, therefore, as in the best concrete poetry, become barely separable from sound and meaning; meaning is 'significantly' tied to voice and appearance, paradoxically at its most acute when presented in the form of a puzzle. Banal though it may be to say that Selerie is primarily a poet of words and meanings, his interest in the history of ciphers, signs, alphabets, orthography, dialect, geometry, algebraic notation, and patterns springs precisely from his engagement with sense rather than being a way of confounding or transcending it. If there are many instances in *Hariot Double* in which poems are hermeneutically obtuse or hermetically opaque, it's not because they are performing exercises in homage to Schwitters or Cobbing, but because they are enjoying the challenges to sense occasioned by diachronic (e.g., archaic diction) and synchronic (e.g., patois) linguistic differences, or because codification and 'noise' (both aurally and visually) play a strong part in the transmission of both arcane and demotic wisdom.

What is both remarkable and perplexing is that this noiseness is introduced into a narrative scenario. Selerie describes his method as 'a dual narrative in fragments'. This is easily accounted for by the influence of Pound and Olson, whose orthographically disturbed long poems, punctuated by

archaic fragments, ideograms and idiolects, form the basis of the modern /
postmodern epic. Yet Selerie draws on these models for intimate excursions
into a fundamentally lyric mode instead of epic extension, and his faith in
the power of association is led by personal, quirky connexions rather than
by the imperatives of cultural critique and historical destining. Olson, as
already mentioned, worked from the local outwards, and his notion of
history is precisely that: finding large-scale resonances in the intimate and
local, his 'method' being *meta hodos*, the path cut not followed. *Hariot
Double* certainly takes off from this principle. And if the narrative idea is
essentially Poundian, its privileging of a kind of archaeological approach to
language owes much to Bunting, whose musical structuring is somehow
not at odds with the injunction to 'take a chisel to write.' Similarly, for
Selerie, 'Poetry is chiselled out of old narratives and faded objects, so as
to create new perspectives and voice structures.' In this recent talk at the
University of London's Senate House, Selerie contends also that '[T]he
search for knowledge – musical, scientific, linguistic – can be compared to
a labyrinth, as Francis Bacon does in the preface to *The Great Instauration*'
and that textual complexity 'may also be regarded as labyrinthine.' Rebecca
Solnit reminds us that 'a labyrinth has only one route, and anyone who
stays with it can find the paradise of the centre and retrace the route to the
exit', unlike mazes, which 'have many branchings and are made to perplex
those who enter.' (*Wanderlust: A History of Walking*, 71) Selerie's heuristic
model, then, is a rational one: his poetic enigmas are meant to resolve into
sense. Yet the diversity of impulses and forms which make up the book are
too mythically arranged to yield to anything like a single narrative goal,
just as the 'metaphysical' bent of the Hariot conjunction never crystallizes
into a clear theme or moral. One graphically inclined form Selerie doesn't
mention is the sixteenth / seventeenth century emblem, and sometimes
individual poems in *Hariot Double* read like emblems without legends,
their picture-text combinations too personally devised to make much
sense. In a recent review, Rupert Loydell complains that *Hariot Double*
is unnecessarily difficult, leaving readers 'outflanked and outmanoeuvred'.
This implies a war between the reader and the poet when I think the worst
that could be said is that it's like a game. To be sure, the text becomes
cryptic, especially at its most calligraphic, and there seems to be a level of
referentiality that is hard to glean. But that's because keeping it strange is
what the documentary poet does. At least unless s/he wants to write an
essay or what Jack Spicer calls 'a letter to the editor'. Loydell wants more
explanation, and there were many times reading this book when I felt a

similar need for something to hold on to. Yet the Poundian insistence is for record and document to be present in their stubborn materiality, so one shouldn't expect a site map. A poem such as 'Mariner's Mirror' is not difficult in terms of its general subject-matter (the moon viewed through a telescope, then compared with the terrestrial world) but in comprehending its precise images and the figurative relationships between them:

> Over this verge, a little ragged, are seas
> I'll hatch or score: ye Caspian, great rug-fleck,
> then below, Foecund and Tranquill
> a jointed arm with tiny ears,
> and either side
> a dream cup and nectar scutch.

Lines cohere soundwise: 'hatch' will be echoed by 'scutch', mediated by 'score' and 'Foecund' and 'cup'. The lyricism is reassuring, by turns mellifluous or crunchy, yet the images drift from easily resolvable ambiguity ('hatch', 'score') to something more recalcitrant: as a verb, to 'scutch' is to separate out the valuable part of a thing from its chaff, which might fit with extracting nectar; as a noun it is the swingling tool itself, or a brick hammer, and also a clump of grass. Nectar scutch seems more of an action than an image as s(c)u(t)ch, and how it connects with 'dream cup' ('cup of dreams'? 'ideal support'?) is anyone's guess. The continuing description of Hariot's diagram shown on the adjacent page resolves into

> a pencil stare into sharper grip
> for any translated spirit

reminding us that, just as in Hariot's day the line between science and the metaphysical was mutable and in the process of being radically redrawn, so poetic language draws on a metaphorical tradition which translates the 'spiritual' into the concrete, and the concrete into abstraction. What is a 'pencil stare'? Etymologically, perhaps, the act of attention through drawing? To stand and stay at attention rather than, say, 'gaze' at the object drawn? At this point, the poem seems less about images than language at its most abstract. While readers might hope that the poem will resolve its documentary sources into a figurative scheme, the documentary element in the facture becomes a knot of linguistic indeterminacy and possibility. The easy way out would be to accept the documentation as simply what it is in its concrete, archaic randomness, yet there's just enough agency in the choice of found text to lure one into the sense of sense. And this is even more so in a more minimalist poem such as 'Cubic Triolet', which demands an organic link between its form and mystical expression: 'not everie part seene / tells its place in here'. The recursive, dialectical rumination is beautifully set in the triolet, yet how does this 'cube' embody 'a bore in a sphere'? A complicating factor is that the geometric and numerical cubes of Hariot's world are associated in the larger scheme of the book with the Harriott poem 'Cane to Cube', where sugar is 'cut into CUBES / all clean & white – empire tight', and there are further metamorphoses into the dice of Harriot's gambling addiction and into his abstract musical shapes (and by extension Selerie's own 'cubism').

The closer contextual proximity of Joe Harriott's world makes for stronger referentiality, but the poems work hard to defamiliarise their documents, and the point again is that Selerie is not looking to translate Harriott's experience into the immediately empathetic but to formalize it. While risking cultural appropriation by using a Jamaican Patois Harriott did not speak publically, he is aware that the poetic rhetoric of simile is a form of assimilation, and therefore avoids the 'relatable' approach of another recent sequence on Harriott, Hannah Lowe's *Chan*. This is not to say that Selerie fails to convey a powerful, immediate sense of Harriott's milieu; on the contrary, Harriott's successes and failures, his passions and anxieties, as well as his life in the London of the '50s and '60s, are documented with great care. But there is a formal distance generated by wordplay and musical equivalence which prevents the poems from becoming an exercise in mimicry and fake authenticity. Harriott's 'voice' shifts between Jamaican English and received orthography. There's nothing patronizing or condescending about the way Selerie channels it, and it's made constantly the subject of self-awareness and cultural difference:

> Plum talk is just the way we got it
> out there. More Britt-ysh in pitch
> than the clipped drawl that toggles
> here.
> ('Tonal')

Formally, again, the Patois connects with Hariot's archaic English and creates a kind of unifying 'free play' for the slang and idiosyncratic diction displayed throughout the book. Nothing is systematic, and the pidgin is complemented by poems that would not be out of place in *Chan*:

> If you've got big hands you struggle
> to get from one note to another.
> I'm sliding around, missing a key
> here and there.
>
> ('Mark 6')

and poems that are in another place altogether:

> They're naked and they dance (40 watt orange bulb,
> broken kitchen chairs). Swedish lessons, phone GER
> 6651 (smeared window). Young girl seeks
> unusual position (baize board). Lady-owner driver
> offers fast sports job (blind alley)…
>
> ('Turf Aslant')

If I understand it, not understanding and the possibility of misunderstanding are a constituent of the poetic strategy. This is not a simple matter of textual obscurity but a crucial factor in what brings together the pieces of the book: Hariot's mathematical discourse, his wordplay and 'universall Alphabet' of Algonkian (which John Aubrey thought devilish), Harriott's scat, and his experiments at the limits of the jazz idiom; the ideological and physical damage caused by mistranslation and appropriation in the colonial and post-colonial settings of Ireland, America, and Britain: 'They think it god-worke.'

Like Allen Fisher, Selerie chivvies his readers to research, yet there is always the 'sense' that no amount of delving will bring them closer to the poetic translation of the source material. You feel that Selerie is a poet strongly in control of his material and that he owns notebooks in which every sign, every quotation and allusion, is carefully logged. Yet none of that tells us very much about the poem as poem. It's useful for the biographer trying to fit an oeuvre to the human subject who created it, but again the presumption is one of rational totality, when the reality is that poets are always writing lines they can't remember having written and can't explain. Such negative capability demands a reader keen to make it all cohere yet unfazed by chance and meaninglessness. In the process, you learn about language itself more than the subject matter, its slipperiness, its musicality, its design, but none of this would happen without the drive to meaning and reference. Ultimately we're responding to imagination over explanation. Picasso said (I learn from a wireless discussion of *Guernica*) that the finished painting is a dead painting, and what I find disappointing in the work of 'mainstream' poets is exactly this drive to finish and to comment on completeness, usually in an elegiac tone. It's as if, in order to comply with the directive of 'serious literature', the poem has to die and in its sighing end explain its existence and existence in general. Which in a sense, a very big sense, is true – at least it's true when Frost makes a whole poem like 'Stopping by Woods on a Snowy Evening' the subject of exquisitely shrouded and illuminated fatalism. But it is not true when in countless Faber-esque jeremiads it becomes an empty reflex, a form of positive incapability. Selerie's achievement is to lead his readers a very long way from this kind of bogus authenticity and toward an exhilarating if sometimes mystifying focus on recalcitrant idioms. He jams together a variety of poetic responses to disparately connected subjects, forming a completeness of artifice while maintaining an horizon of incompleteness, allowing free play within a tightly organized conceptual structure.

Simon Smith

Tilting Forward Lift

(for Gavin Selerie)

Therefore, the flower & the word for flower vibrate. Dice thrown in & to the rim, agile & form. Who are we meeting ourselves going back? Timed, analogue. My father a star in the anagram, glass to glance. Pages creased, faded & folded, blank transparencies, patterning looked after.

Nets like hair, braids & micro plastics, stripped down to the granular data, to translation – to move over water, the seabed, the shadow of form. With a stopwatch I'm singing to the chorus – who are you left, eating dust? Mouthing the turn turning diagonal, square or pentagon, tilting?

The satellite crashed into the comet's surface – the full Moon layered with impacts, Jupiter spinning atop, like a two-way bet with ray-guns – canals, veins, arteries – the to & fro, the heart & out – to turn the diamond point true to the book of pure sound into a dice roll, a therefore.

Therefore, what the calyx protects, what rattles with Indian waves are mirrors like star jumps, sign in at the sign of the swan, haunted by the anagram, hearing my heartbeat, pump blood through the ear: ear – hear – heart & sideways: my conscience, my coincidence with the World.

Therefore, we exist in between earth & sky in slim glitter. Dream of a minute a minute. The eyes are mirrors. The clock echoes time, the passage, the page a mirage. Each frame bleached of colour face up in the burning light, the pure eternal present, the pure anagram the sign sings.

In this envelope of undoing in between unfinished & one voice of attachment; dice the absolute contingent, midnight marked as time, then one minute past. Blank layout – blank – blank – blank, frame by frame, black & white, blinding & binary, hearing my heartbeat back to myself.

Father on a journey to another star passes close by – Orion, Sirius, the Great Bear, vagrant, vagabond performer. Blue & orange flame of dawn. What dies in the Indies – over horizon operations – tilt into the cloud to play the chord. Currents & tides. On your way. Hauntology.

Rhythm between objects your mouth floats yeses, strings of the small, repeated days. Analogue. Switches & buttons. Page as hinge to gape, sign in & sing, the cold sinking. I am made of code. When gazing into the mirror I am there. & not there. Touch & off. Binary. Dispossessed.

Therefore, beauty & then idea, the blanks & the blancs folded the voice back in the book. The me abandoned, line stretched over line to carry the astringent, the argument, the sonnet the room to dwell in. My blood count counting. From the eyes to hearsay, my speaking. Hauntingly.

I'm singing in the chorus how are you? Is to say your move. Structure over organic form, the hook celebrates the word, the love in the song. Cup to toast, cup to dice, & the sound of elsewhere. Peek from behind fingers, when tipped up into the mirror there you go, disappeared.

Therefore, in the conjunctions, the thresholds, the hinge, the meetings shaken in the cup, signing & singing. We extend ourselves into the actual, diced, gear change in the anagram – the time come in the anagram close by the doorway, tilting forward to be in love with the World.

October 2022

Matt Martin

gallimawfrey

with the York poems in Gavin Selerie's *Azimuth*
(London: Binnacle Press, 1984)

buried in the dark, an age	'oled in't' pit mirk an eld
the whole world alive as today	all-'ow-an'-abaht-it on life like terday
start with the sun, and the rest	set agate wit' skrike uv day
will slowly happen	an't remblent throo time cums o'er
the ground blackened hard	t'flat bark'd inonder't'
beneath a crust of ice	screefs uv ist
at the end of a walk,	ut ootrake's lappin'-up
in the chill air, the wheels turn	in't' slythe
endlessly on nothing	quells welt baht lin on't' nowt
my house	me hemble 'olds feet
is outside the city walls,	aht yond tahn brest
and they close the gates at dusk	an't' bars git fast ut darklin'
sometimes I think there's nothing	oddlins ah reckon there bain't nowt
but a warm body close to earth	baht yattish soul-case ligg'd nigh acker
squatted the land and lived	liv'd upright ut unthank
by the old tongue and by candlelight	bah t'aud-farand twang 'n' tapett-flowers
I am a star(ling)	missen a shep
that wanders with you	at flizzes wit' tha
as lush fields roll over	as hade on't' howmy hade swallops
sand and gravel	o'er't' yeller grout
a willow and ash	a wilf 'n' esh
marking the limits	metin'
of verdure	vert's mere

find daffodils, a splash of gold	meet daffodowndillies
on the green rampart	swattlin' nobles on't grosk batter
people pushing with fervour	ingangers anonskerly possin'
till they're ready to drop, like fish	while they's pagger'd aht, like dogdraves
piled in baskets on the river bank	ruck'd in't' leaps on't' watterbank
a drill pounding	a stane-joss brayin'
to get even with the juggernauts,	ter let bound wains know what's t'matter
scaffolding all around	scatches round an' sware
the sun cuts dust, traces	kims prick a flisk
a pageant on flagstones	on't' flags
people and their makings	canthrifs an' their dazzity
come real through corruption	o'erlive pash
in the good intentions of each other	in tentin' tane-t'uther

Alan Halsey

Maze for Grammatologists

Printed on the cover of Shearsman *magazine, 1st series, #7 (1982).*

Lightning Source UK Ltd.
Milton Keynes UK
UKHW010750151222
413978UK00001B/95

9 781848 618732